Liberating
Black
Church
History

Liberating Black Church History

Juan M. Floyd-Thomas

Abingdon Press

Nashville

LIBERATING BLACK CHURCH HISTORY:
MAKING IT PLAIN
Copyright © 2014 by Abingdon Press

This book is printed on acid-free paper.

Library of Congress Cataloging-in-Publication Data

Floyd-Thomas, Juan Marcial.
  Liberating black church history : making it plain / Juan M. Floyd-Thomas.
    pages cm
  Includes bibliographical references.
  ISBN 978-0-687-33275-5 (trade pbk., adhesive perfect binding, soft back : alk. paper) 1. Black theol-
ogy—History. 2. African American churches—History. 3. United States—Church history. I. Title.
  BT82.7.F56 2014
  277.30089'96073—dc23

                                                                                              2013046544

14 15 16 17 18 19 20 21 22 23—10 9 8 7 6 5 4 3 2 1
MANUFACTURED IN THE UNITED STATES OF AMERICA

To my dearest Stacey

CONTENTS

ACKNOWLEDGMENTS

Without question, writing a book is an elaborate process that typically consists of varying degrees of inspiration, frustration, perspiration, and determination, but rarely is it ever done in isolation. I want to thank my editor at Abingdon Press, Kathy Armistead, who did an exceptional job bringing this book to fruition. What most impressed me about working with Kathy was how deeply concerned she was about the project from its title to its main themes to its cover art. Her passionate commitment to this project kept me motivated to seeing the work to its completion. I am also grateful for Kelsey Spinnato, who copyedited the manuscript as well as guided the book through the final stages of production. Her straightforward attention to detail and evenhanded approach to the logistical details of the publishing process have been invaluable. I also reserve special thanks for Bob Ratcliff and John Kutsko who were instrumental to this volume's inception during their tenure at Abingdon, and I am grateful for their friendship for more than a decade.

While researching and writing this book, I have been blessed with the support of colleagues, friends, and family too numerous to mention, but I would like to acknowledge a few individuals here. During the earliest stages of research and writing for this project, conversations with Barbara D. Savage, A. G. Miller, Vincent Harding, William R. Jones, Peter Paris, Renita Weems, Alton B. Pollard III, James Cone, Teresa Fry Brown, Dennis Wiley, M. Shawn Copeland, Martha Simmons, and Forrest E. Harris Sr. all along the way were especially helpful to bringing added dimensions and energy to this endeavor for which I am extremely thankful. I am also grateful for the seminarians and graduate students at Vanderbilt Divinity School whose thoughtful questions and critical engagement have constantly challenged me to think more deeply and write more clearly about African American religious history. A note of special thanks to Rev. Dr. Frederick Douglass Haynes III, senior pastor of Friendship West Baptist Church of Dallas, Texas, for unwavering encouragement at critical stages of this book's development that ultimately proved indispensible, and I will be eternally grateful to him as both a pastor and friend. With a tremendous generosity of intellect and willingness of spirit, Anthony Pinn, David Nelson, and Herbert Marbury each read early drafts of the manuscript and helped me to make corrections and additions that ultimately reshaped the contours of the book into its current iteration.

Meanwhile, no words can adequately express how much love and support I received during the unexpectedly long gestation period of this project and every endeavor. My mother, Desrine Thomas, taught me to believe that all things are possible with hard work and determination, and I am endlessly grateful for her insights. I also want to express my appreciation to Lillian Floyd and Janet Floyd, my mother-in-law and sister-in-law respectively, who have contributed greatly to my efforts in countless ways.

Finally, I leave my deepest and most heartfelt gratitude to my wife, Stacey Floyd-Thomas, and our daughter, Lillian. I dedicated the book to Stacey because no one is more responsible for this book's existence than she is. Aside from reading numerous revisions of the manuscript and offering thoughtful feedback, Stacey's steadfast faith, abiding love, and boundless wisdom always kept me grounded. Our beautiful and brilliant daughter, Lillian, is simply the most remarkable individual I have ever known because of her infinite ability to find new ways to make me think, laugh, and truly appreciate the extraordinary world in which we live. More than anything, I hope to be as much a symbol of God's love and grace in their lives as they are in mine.

INTRODUCTION

Lessons the Dark Past Has Taught Me

Research is formalized curiosity. It is poking and prying with a purpose.

Zora Neale Hurston

I have been enamored by the study of history since my childhood. When I was about ten years old, my mother enrolled in a nursing program at the local college. To my young mind, she brought what seemed to be an endless supply of books into our home based on whatever courses she was taking at the time. Being a curious, rather precocious child raised in a single-parent household, I was intrigued by these strange books that my mother focused upon so intently (like many children, looking at these presumably adult reading materials was somewhat exhilarating for me). While I found her math and science textbooks unappealing, I stumbled upon a stash of books that grabbed my attention immediately and intensely. On a bookshelf in the guest bedroom, there was an old copy of *The Autobiography of Malcolm X* with a classic black-and-white snapshot of Malcolm X with an enraged look on his face and his index finger wagging in stern consternation on the book's cover. This image captured my attention until I felt compelled to flip the pages of the book. Without any truly sophisticated idea of who Malcolm X was either on his own terms or in comparison with Rev. Dr. Martin Luther King Jr. (this was years before I knew of

James Cone's theological reflections about these two prophetic figures), I was mesmerized by the depth of Malcolm's life experiences as a young Black man trying to achieve his sense of God-given purpose in spite of a dizzying array of hardships—racism, poverty, mental illness, miseducation, religious doubt, drug abuse, criminality, and so on. This discovery struck a deep chord inside me. Years later I learned of a quote by Malcolm X that has since captivated me, namely, the statement that "of all our studies, history is best qualified to reward our research." What I did not know then but understand now is that I was most fascinated by this acclaimed memoir of the slain leader because, by reading every word on the printed page, I slowly learned what it meant to live with and actually love history.

After reading that book, I became an avid reader, especially of works that I considered "historical." As I put aside my boyhood comic books and started raiding my mother's book collection, the books that arrested my gaze and would not let me rest until I read them were Alex Haley's *Roots* and Ralph Ellison's *Invisible Man*, as well as a volume of Edward Gibbons's *The Rise and Fall of the Roman Empire*. All of these works cannot be strictly classified as historical in any traditional sense. However, all of these books awakened my young mind to the wealth of knowledge about the overall human condition that can be gained by reading about the lives and times of others. Unbeknownst to either me or my mother, having those books within reach ignited my lifelong enthusiasm for history that later led to my decision to study history from the first day of my undergraduate years to graduate school and beyond.

I share this anecdote against all personal instincts and professional inclinations in order to make one point perfectly clear: how one envisions and ultimately engages with history begins at home and with family. Although my parents separated and eventually divorced, they remained united and interested in my literacy. In turn, I translated their concern about my education into a youthful enthusiasm for history. Before any schoolteacher, guidance counselor, or principal made a formal attempt to nurture this sensibility in me, the opportunity to read and reflect on these works was only possible because I had an environment at home that encouraged me to read everything I could get my hands on—the more esoteric and obscure, the better. But rather than grapple with history as some lonely, isolating endeavor, I found the ability to learn about all sorts of people, living and dead, who piqued my interest in a variety of ways: the famous and the infamous; men and women; descendants of Africa, Europe, and the New World; Christians and non-Christians; the mighty and the meek. It is through surveying this rich panorama of history that I became concerned about the power of narrative and exposition. In other words, approaching history in a serious fashion meant nurturing a great adoration for the construction and rendition of a good story.

When thinking about the shortcomings most Black people encounter in their relationship with history, I often think of philosopher Cornel West's concept of nihilism, which he envisions as "a natural consequence of a culture (or civilization) ruled and regulated by categories that mask manipulation, mastery and domination of peoples and nature." Defined as "the lived experience of coping with a life of horrifying meaninglessness, hopelessness, and (most important) lovelessness," West's understanding of nihilism is a truly invaluable way of facing the great chasm that many Black people feel exists between themselves and the historical past.[1] Put another way, nihilism manifests itself as a great sadness borne of helplessness on one hand and hopelessness on the other that creates a palpable pain and a venerable vulnerability that inhabits the heart of Black history. Nevertheless, because of the omnipresent pain and shame of slavery and the persistent trauma of anti-Black racism in its myriad forms, too many Black people consider history something to be *escaped* rather than *embraced*. In thinking historically, we have to approach history as a means of personal and collective liberation. Conversely, taking away a people's history is a means of enslaving them. Thus, history is a double-edged sword that can be used either to oppress or to liberate Black folks. However, in the face of this dual tension, there is the existential crisis at the core of the Black experience. This book intends to help rectify this matter.

During introductory class meetings, I typically instruct my students that history is a study of the PAST. In this instance, the term *PAST*—principles, assumptions, society, and transitions—is used as an acronym and a mnemonic device to reflect the key categorical concerns that arguably comprise the structural core of historical knowledge and experience. As the first of these categorical concerns, *principles* reflect the ideas, values, philosophy, and ethics that shape and guide the means by which we achieve some semblance of human coexistence in the world. Second, *assumptions* address the myths, symbolic images, stereotypes, and generalized perspectives at various levels of consciousness to comprise the common-sense narrative that lies at the heart of human history. Next, *society* refers to the aggregate people, institutions, and culture that comprise our corporate reality as both social and sentient creatures. Finally, *transitions* indicate not only how human beings move through time, space, and circumstance but also how people negotiate varying conflicts over differing interests and competing needs. Taken as a whole, thinking of the historic past in this fashion helps one overcome the mundane misconception prevalent within contemporary popular thought that the discipline of history is simply an arduous ordeal full of names, dates, places, and statistics ready for rote memorization and uncritical regurgitation.

Without fail, many of us are drawn to certain events, topics, images, figures, and questions because they tend to say something about our identity and experience. Put another way, *what* we choose to notice about the past, *where* we find our facts, and *why* we do so says something intrinsically about *who* we are today and *how* we see ourselves in the broad sense of human existence. Finding approaches that enable anyone interested in African American religious history to live with and love the subject matter at hand involves making specific (sometimes strategic) choices about who or what to remember or who or what to recall.

Many disciplinary gatekeepers would assert that such a claim sets loose reckless moles of revisionists who will tear down the protective walls of the historical profession. What such thinking does is create a siege mentality wherein historical knowledge is treated as a rarified (and in too many cases, fossilized) relic that can only be handled by a select (or dare I say "the Elect") few. This betrays the core belief of this field of human inquiry that I acquired at the feet of numerous historians and other scholars who were impassioned by the prospect of cultivating what they succinctly called "the usable past." This notion of a usable past—an academic product of the intellectual, sociopolitical, and spiritual forces that came together in the red-hot crucible of 1960s democratic idealism—spoke to the reality that although only a handful of people might be able to skillfully produce and manage chronicles of the human past, everyone has stake in fair and equal ownership of history. In that spirit, history ought to be regarded as both a communal enterprise and a collective resource that involves widening our vistas of the human experience that can start at home but do not stay there exclusively or eternally.

In terms of African American religious history, when and where we enter the story based on our particular identity and circumstances (race, gender, class, religion, ethnicity, nationality, sexuality, age, and so on) should allow individuals and groups to eventually see what all human beings ultimately share in common. In many regards, I liken this to James Cone's assertion that

> while we must begin our theological reflection with the particularity of our own struggle for justice, we should never stop there. The truth of our particular struggle pushes us beyond ourselves to the truth of other struggles.[2]

In other words, by exploring the depths of the specific, we should be able to uncover the mysteries of the universal.

When history is thoughtfully and carefully constructed, it does not have to be exclusive in its vision or narrowly parochial in nature. In an era wherein both sides of the nation's culture wars want to proclaim we are in a post-everything moment and their side won (regardless of actual facts to the contrary on either side), history has such great potential for us and our world. Knowledge of history in its truest sense invites us to understand other people, places, and times and, in so doing, to put our innate assumptions about the historicized Other to the test. Moreover, gleaning the existence of triumphs and tragedies that are rooted in and yet transcend the experiences of diverse languages, cultures, and circumstances from different times and regions can contribute to creating a shared sensitivity and compassion among peoples both intra- and interracially that exceed the token gestures of multiculturalism and political correctness. Remembering previous times of abundance or recalling earlier times of adversity is the vital thread of history because it allows us to draw consolation from the past and offer hope for the present in order to help us imagine the future. As noted historian Vincent Harding argues, "The story of the African American struggle for freedom, democracy and transformation is a great, continuing human classic whose liberating lessons are available to all," especially those who are willing to struggle and sacrifice for the creation of a better society and a more hopeful world.[3] This concern is the crux of this book.

At this point, it seems only right to explain the significance of the title of this volume, *Liberating Black Church History: Making It Plain.* Like many things, the title lends itself to many interpretations and inflections based on one's particular point of view or desired approach to the text. To begin the process of making sense of this text, let us first pay attention to the phrase *making it plain.* Armed with the clarity of historical perspective, we can also deflate the self-absorption and arrogance that drives much of our society's present-mindedness and cultural myopia by allowing us to see old problems in a new light. Looking backward expands our vision, allowing us to keep our attention on the problems, prayers, progress, and promises of our forebears. In countless ways, the tableau of African American religious history reflects a diverse tapestry of spirit-filled people striving—although not always succeeding—to stay in faithful and fruitful right relationship with one another, their ancestors, and God.

Although the history of Black Christianity has often been portrayed as being quite conservative and traditional in both thought and practice, liberation has been the central theme of Black religious life. The novelist and social critic James Baldwin once said, "If the concept of God has any use, it is to make us larger, freer, and more loving."[4] Time and time again, it has been not only important but also necessary for us to reexamine our basic assumptions by reframing Baldwin's comment into a series of questions to provide opportunities for deeper, more thorough introspection about our own notions of our faith and spirituality. Therefore, following Baldwin's line of reasoning, one might ponder, "How might the concept of God, as well as God's ontology, be used to make us larger, freer, and more loving?" Embedded within this query is a series of equally pressing quandaries that have to be addressed in order to make sense of the history of Black Christian thought in the modern world, namely: Who is the God that we call God? How do we imagine this God, and how does that affect our experience of that God? And, in turn, our relationships with one another and ourselves? When it is all said and done, it seems that, in order for the concept of God to be used to the ends that Baldwin suggests, we need to consider another essential question: Is the historical image of God within the Black Christian tradition one that has been both liberating and loving? This also seems to be at the heart of Christ's message—to make a truly flawed and perfectly imperfect humanity larger, freer, and more loving through God's salvific power, grace, and mercy. When the title talks about "liberating Black Church history," it is intentionally and ideally grappling with answering this set of profound and provocative questions.

Whereas Black Christians have certainly affirmed the traditional beliefs of the church universal, the reality is that spiritual faith for Americans of African descent over several centuries has been rooted in a movement from slavery to freedom, both literally and figuratively. For the typical churchgoer in the pew of a historically African American church, the term *keeping the faith* means more than just maintaining the consistency and constancy of one's prayer life and devotional practices but also holding a deep conviction that through God's grace, love, and mercy, tomorrow can be better than yesterday.

Historically, Black churches have been a place to which African Americans could escape from their oppression and dehumanization by white people. In these sacred houses of worship, it has been preached, prayed, and sung that "everybody is somebody in God's eyes even if you're considered nobody here on Earth!" From their earliest roots in North America more than two hundred years ago until now, Black churches still offer believers this spiritual message of liberty, empowerment, and affirmation. But even when the theological message has been focused on otherworldly escape with a fixation on the heavenly promise of freedom in the afterlife more than struggling for freedom in the earthly realm, the church has been a refuge and safe haven for healing. Moreover, the church has proven itself even in the worst moments of the African American experience, where it enabled Black Christians to remain sane in the midst of the sheer insanity of chattel slavery and the utter absurdity of Jim and Jane Crow segregation. The premise of being a "somebody in God's eyes" is a powerful incentive to work toward remaking a vision of society that validates the human dignity of everyone.

Arguably, the most distinctive contribution of the Black Church tradition to the mainline American theological enterprise has been Black liberation theology. Without question, Black theology is not merely normative Christian theology (i.e., a perspective that is overwhelmingly elite, white, Western European, and male in nature) rendered in blackface or sepia-tone. Instead, the experience of Blackness has guided, informed, and influenced the history of Black Christian thought right from the very beginning. The African American Christian experience sets the agenda for this way of doing theology both in church and society. As theologian James Cone writes:

> I still regard the Bible as an important source of my theological reflections, but not the starting point. The black experience and the Bible together in dialectical tension serve as my point of departure. . . . The order is significant. I am *black* first—and everything else comes after that. This means that I read the Bible through the lens of a black tradition and not as the objective word of God.[5]

There are a number of themes upon which nearly all Black liberation theologians would agree, namely, freedom, justice, and equality. For instance, as sociologists C. Eric Lincoln and Lawrence Mamiya state it, "The Old Testament notion of God as an avenging, conquering, liberating paladin remains a formidable anchor of faith." However, the vision of Jesus as the liberator of the poor and oppressed Black masses is unquestionably the controlling theme of Black liberation theology. The suffering of Black people throughout their history finds "immediate resonance with the incarnational view of the suffering, humiliation, death, and eventual triumph of Jesus in the resurrection."[6] To this point, much of Black religious thought draws upon both the Hebrew Bible and Christian New Testament yet redefines Jesus Christ as liberator in terms of seeking better prospects for life and love in the modern world such as jobs, equal access to educational opportunities, voting rights, adequate housing, and affordable health care. The liberation that Jesus offers certainly includes freedom from the eternal punishment of unforgiven sin. It certainly includes a hoped-for future in which oppression and pain of every kind shall cease. But first and foremost, Jesus Christ means liberation now in sociopolitical and economic dimensions. In other words, Jesus means full humanity for those who have never known it for themselves.

Black liberation theology also emphasizes that justice is part of the eternal nature of God, especially with regard to the fate of the marginalized and downtrodden. This liberationist viewpoint espouses that God is on the side of the oppressed and against the oppressors. In this reading of both history and faith, God does not support the authority of the ruling class and the dominance of the status quo but rather the Divine supports the attempt to bring about a more just and equal society. This notion of divine justice, too, reflects the power and importance of the prophetic books of the Hebrew Bible in Black religiosity. In a similar vein, the kingdom and kin-dom of God[7] is seen in terms of securing the blessings of freedom, justice, and equality in this world. The liberationist perspective encourages Black Christians to be responsible for bringing it about in the world with God's help and guidance. Although such pure and perfect liberty may not come into its fullness until God intervenes directly and decisively in human affairs, human heads, hearts, and hands can greatly advance the work of liberation. Without a shadow of a doubt, Black liberation theology is a theology of political action wherein concepts such as the kingdom and kin-dom of God are consciously used as political constructs, which are meant to be translated into concrete changes in how people live out their daily lives.

Moreover, Black religious thought is thoroughly contextual. As suggested above, normative Christian theology has usually been done by and for the benefit of privileged white men. It has usually been assumed that there was but one theology with no room for alternate visions or considerations. At its best, contextual theology recognizes that even though all Christians believe that there is only one God, there are a vast number of ways that believers may understand and envision God for themselves, based on their era, cultural heritage, and existential experience. Theology is a circular process in which the current situation and the Bible are used to interpret and reinterpret each other. Therefore, for Black liberation theology, the starting point is always the collective experience of slavery and segregation. When seen in this light, any theology that does not take that historical experience into account and does not ring true to those people whose entire identity and frame of cultural reference is marked by that selfsame experience can never be considered valid.

Although often obscured in the traditional annals of church history, it must never be forgotten that Black liberation theology was the first of the contextual, liberation-oriented theologies to emerge in the United States during the last half-century. Undeniably, the pioneering work of Black liberation theologians—whether in church sanctuaries, in seminary classrooms, or on city streets—helped all theologians both in the United States and beyond begin to realize just how people's social location and cultural background deeply informed their theological perspective. Once it garnered widespread attention, Black liberation theology clearly set the stage for subsequent efforts across the spectrum of racial, ethnic, gender, sexual, class-based, and national identities to interpret the Christian message in terms of linking theology to the specificity of a particular people's history. This development has definitely made it much more difficult to simply go back to business as usual and justify the study of Christian thought and practice as if time, place, culture, and circumstance do not exist or never mattered. Therefore, in a great hope to return the favor, this volume intends to raise key issues and critical insights within the broad history of the Black Church tradition as viewed through the perspectival lens of Black liberation theology.

The key to understanding why history matters is to strip away all preconceived notions and prejudices about it as a discipline and redefine it in a way that gives it a new, more purposeful meaning—in other words, *make it plain*. So, when talking about history in a practical sense, it is simply the formalized process of recording what has happened for the sake of remembering who we have been, how we have been, and most important, why we have been in a certain point in time and place. Central to the historical enterprise is the act of calling back to one's remembrance the people, issues, places, and experiences that have or impart meaning for our lives. When considering the "story" embedded within the word *history*, it is necessary to realize how much of what we remember or recall is transmitted from one generation to the next, whether it is the memory (no matter how sloppy or selective) of major turning points, legendary individuals, or transformative instances of great joy or profound terror.

MEMORY AS A MATTER OF FAITH AND HISTORY

Without question, memory is one of the most powerful facets of the human condition. One of the most noteworthy reflections on memory can be found in the writings of Augustine. In his *Confessions*, the influential fourth-century North African theologian refers to memory as the "vast court" that holds the "treasury" in the mind. From this perspective, Augustine stands awestruck by the sheer force of memory, calling it a great "chamber" of which no one had "sounded the bottom thereof." "Great is the power of memory," Augustine writes, "a fearful thing. O my God, a deep and boundless manifoldness; and this thing is the mind, and this am I myself."[8] Embedded within his statement, it is evident that Augustine is convinced that our memories are the core of our identities. Of course, all of us have memory lapses or worry when our ability to recall the past comes up short. Moreover, in spite of our best efforts, we live a sociocultural context in which a genuine appreciation of history is undervalued at best and undermined at worst for the majority of students in the American educational system from kindergarten to college.[9]

Bad as this predicament is for all Americans, this problem of losing history is of particular concern for Black people. From that standpoint, what constitutes a "good" memory? Similarly, many of us fret about our memory as we grow older or about our lives becoming more frantic in nature. I will admit that, even as a historian, I wonder about the sublime mystery of human memory that makes it possible for me to recall the chronology of Dr. Martin Luther King Jr.'s leadership of the civil rights movement or arcane details about the Councils of Chalcedon or Nicaea but to misplace my car keys or to utterly forget items from my grocery list. Another intriguing facet of growing older is that I realize that most of my waking thoughts are more often than not becoming memories of memories rather than recollection of actual past events.

In ways too numerous to count or predict, these intangible and ephemeral processes of retaining and recalling past experience dictate to each of us who and how we should be. Conversely, it can be argued that as our memories begin to take shape and serve to define the essence of our being, we respond to them. As a consequence, we end up spending much of our finite human existence ceaselessly trying to either revive or revise them. On the one hand, memory not only can dominate our thoughts but also can threaten to subdue and even ruin us. On the other hand, the persistence of memory also has the power to save us from absolute confusion and utter despair. As a central paradox of the human condition, it is part of our burdensome agony to live with our memories as well as to realize that in the final analysis, we also cannot live without this blessed gift.

To make this point more forcefully, despite the struggle, we all have to try and remember that things of varying importance essentially obscure a cardinal truth: history *is not* and *never has been* simply about rote memorization. Books and their electronic/digital counterparts are conveniently portable and tangible mnemonic implements that allow us to look up accurate information about dates, names, essential terms, and important issues (with correct spellings and grammatical sense no less). While this might seem painfully obvious to some readers, there are many students, especially adult learners returning to the classroom after being away for any number of years, who view books as daunting, intimidating things. Overcoming such self-imposed obstacles is a liberating step toward cultivating one's own system of remembering. In this sense, history—much like life itself—is what you make it. Therefore, each person ought to use whatever means work best.

Hence, as a facet of historical knowledge, having a "good" memory is only as significant as what we choose to recall or recite. Facing the realization that human memory is unwavering in its fallibility and selectivity is often pigeonholed in terms of what we can successfully memorize and what eventually surfaces as we are able to eventually recall. In sum, history is not about regurgitating a list of names or rattling off a time line of events without any sense of their connection. Instead, the meaning of history has everything to do with sharing stories and sentiments that resonate in the very core of our beings and help make us who we are for better or worse. When asked, most people can remember not just the names or faces but also the feelings evoked by loved ones, even those whom they have not seen for years or who might have been deceased a long time. In those moments, in which memories might occasionally falter, being able to gaze at family keepsakes or old photos brings memories rushing forth.

WRITING A HISTORY OF BLACK FAITH

Caught between the polar extremes of despair and hope, African Americans continue to face stark situations with a steady and abiding religious faith. The national trends and social indicators all suggest the utter collapse of Black poor and working-class communities on political and economic levels that worsen with each passing day. Illegal drug abuse continues to plague countless communities while various forms of unchecked violence toward and among African Americans continue to escalate to levels that have never before been witnessed. Single-parent households continue to be inordinately prevalent in African American families since the publication of the infamous Moynihan Report in 1965. The expanded number of African Americans imprisoned within state and federal correctional institutions far exceeds the total number of enslaved Black men in the 1850s and the number of Blacks presently enrolled in colleges. In the wake of the catastrophic aftermath of Hurricane Katrina in 2005, the nation finally awakened to the fact that the structural realities of Black poverty and homelessness have severely deepened in the last decade.

On the whole, statistics of human misery and social devastation were not caused by accident or from some lack of a work ethic among African Americans. Arguably these issues were the direct results of deliberate governmental and corporate policies in an era that was supposed to be defined by key buzzwords such as *compassionate conservatism*, *value voters*, and *faith-based initiatives*. Meanwhile, the legacy of the civil rights movement no longer assumes that the oppression and subjugation of people of color, especially Blacks, has ended, but rather it now seems that hate crimes and racial slurs can rule the day in the crudest, most racist terms. In such a context, African Americans need to ponder whether the resurgence of a religious faith that transcends these contemporary dilemmas can also instill a greater sense of destiny.

FAITH IN BLACK CHURCH HISTORY

Posing questions is the primary means of learning history for oneself. When reading a work of history, here are some of the questions the reader needs to ask: Who is the author? What is he or she trying to accomplish with this text? From what perspective is he or she writing? To what audience or community is the author writing? Moving beyond these preliminary questions, the historical method requires a level of curiosity that will allow the reader to engage the text and the represented sources with queries that increasingly probe. For instance, it is important that a reader understands where a historian decides to begin and end a particular story because it can be quite illuminating. When reading a historical text, it is always worthwhile to think about who is present in the text as well as who is rendered absent or nonexistent in this particular account.

When examining any historical account, there has to be a cognizance of who is present in the text and who is not. Or does this historian's work challenge my preconceived notions and force me to sharpen my own thinking? From the vantage point of Black people, a historical text is judged by how it depicts people of African descent. Any diligent reader of historical research ought to be equally moved no matter who is represented, whether children, the elderly, the middle-aged, the enslaved, the emancipated, women, men, the poor or wealthy, or the disadvantaged or the privileged. When reading a given text, the reader has to wonder whose transcripts and testimonies are given more emphasis and consideration. In these and many other ways, an insightful reading is comparable to biblical criticism. Much like one might explore and exegete scriptures, reading religious history in a critical fashion means that readers ask questions about the known past as informed by the present as a means of acquiring wisdom for the future. In this regard, the historian wrestles with how faith is revealed or expressed.

As important as posing questions are to *reading* history, knowing what questions to ask is indispensable to *writing* history. When beginning to craft a narrative about a particular subject, the historian needs to pose crucial questions such as: "What happened next? Who was there? Who was not? Why? Why not?" Such probing queries are required to chart the direction of the research as well as to move the story forward. As mentioned earlier, a healthy dose of curiosity is mandatory for historical writing because it shapes and guides the historian's focus and enables her to identify familiar sources, to ignore the extraneous or irrelevant, and to interrogate new, previously unknown information.

The lynchpin of historical methodology is found in the process of following the trail of documentary evidence and pursuing the resulting story wherever it leads. In a classic treatise, historian Robin Winks once likened the work of the professional historian to being a detective.[10] The analogy to detective work reflects the keen awareness that following the story to its most logical and objective ends is part and parcel of the disciplinary training and vital labor of the historian. Based on the preparation, personal passion, and pressing questions that compel historians to select a given subject for their work, the dual intention of historical writing is to uncover new evidence and unfold the narrative in an engaging manner.

The enterprise of historical research is both imaginative and scientific in nature. Furthermore, rigorous, insightful research is necessary to support the historian's consideration of past events. History is multidimensional in its methodology and approach to the past. By extension, historians specialize in weaving together accounts of the past from divergent and often contradictory primary and secondary written, oral, and visual source materials. Within the scope of any historiographical project, private recollections and public documents vie for a fine balance between authority and priority. When thinking of history as an art and science, there must be an organic synergy between the two.

For example, let us think about the balance between stories and statistics within the historical enterprise. On the one hand, statistics and other modes of data analysis can provide helpful and critical proof to a world bound by structural inequalities and gagged by generational silences. Sociologist C. Wright Mills says that social research is often driven by the interplay of public issues and private troubles. In that sense, what might initially seem like sterile trivia and alien factoids, when the social problem seeking resolution becomes *your* problem, no bit of information can be considered too minute or arcane if it holds the key to unlocking your destiny. On the other hand, people respond to stories not just to statistics. A flood of information can sweep away everything in its path yet never change the world one iota. Statistics are best expressed and remembered by the reader when the researcher couches them in a context of some sense of allegory, metaphor, memory, or drama. Conversely, a story can enliven the spirit, enlighten the mind, and empower a person, showing that there may be, in fact, a way forward beyond the gloom and doom often indicated by statistical data. A history that has any meaning and power in this world must be engagingly focused on objective thinking and empathetic feeling about the past in order to inform the present and inspire the future.

Earlier, I emphasized that the reading and writing of history has personal dimensions that might begin in the discovery of past issues, individuals, or events but does not have to remain trapped there. In fact, the great beauty of historical research rests in the way that the deepest yearnings to uncover the unknown past come from the desire to better understand the present and thereby to shape the future. But this comes with a caveat: more people than I care to remember have worn out historian George Santayana's oft-quoted statement—"Those who fail to learn from history are doomed to repeat it"[11]—but miss the point entirely. I ask any person who uses this cliché as a means of demonstrating his or her "savvy" on all historical matters, how many times he or she has relived the Haitian Revolution or the Harlem Renaissance. For those who are not quite so literal-minded yet still do not grasp the profundity of what Santayana was originally saying, the point is not that historical situations will actually repeat themselves. To the contrary, no matter how we believe human history unfolds this

16

often-repeated warning lets us know that we can avoid some of the consequences of perennial problems endemic to the human condition—prejudice, war, disease, poverty, famine, crime, despair—if we prepare ourselves by studying the past. Therefore, Santayana's sage advice suggests that historical knowledge can serve as a bulwark against an increasingly uncertain future by providing us a relatively solid foundation of past experiences and proven insights. In turn, once we are fully aware of the past, then and only then can we reasonably engage the future with the guarantee of restored hope, new perspectives, and strategic planning.

An interesting example of how using historical knowledge within the context of the Black Church tradition is evident in the use of the exodus motif by African Americans to reclaim their understanding of the Black freedom struggle in North America. Within the three major epochs of African American history discussed in this book—slavery (1619–1865), segregation (1865–1965), and social disruption (1965–present)—the paradigm of Moses and the Israelites seeking God's intervention to end their unyielding and inhumane bondage in Pharaoh's Egypt has had a resonance for Black folk seeking an end to enslavement and all related forms of crippling oppression. Those enslaved forebears who forged the rudiments of a composite African faith system in the New World, which we call slave religion, often turned to the story of the exodus for divine wisdom and scriptural authority to overcome the tyranny of chattel slavery in antebellum America. Under the yoke of racial segregation, the biblical images and symbolism of the exodus narrative were means of overturning the ravages of Jim and Jane Crow laws that circumscribed Black people's lives and longings to the dictates of white America's whims and wantonness. During the post–civil rights era, however, an intriguing shift took place when Black people endeavored to explore the history of Egypt to face the challenges of a new era. Scholars such as Albert Raboteau, Vincent Harding, and Eddie Glaude looked at the exodus story with fresh eyes and articulated the fundamental paradox of this paradigm: How can America be both Egypt *and* the promised land?[12] Moreover, in the wake of Black biblical criticism and Afrocentricism's arrival in the Academy, the ontology of race, racism, and power that exists in the modern American context gets radically skewed once we look at both the Egyptians and Israelites having common African ancestry.[13] What happens when Black folk see themselves aligned with both the oppressor and the oppressed within the scriptural account? In light of this revelation, is it possible that Black people can envision themselves as both Pharaoh and Moses?

While this certainly does not disqualify how the exodus motif has been used by Black Christians as a means of envisioning liberation, seeing this scriptural narrative in light of new critical frameworks and methodological tools definitely complicates matters and thus gives us cause to think. As this example suggests, we must ask questions as the historical account unfolds in order to gain a sense of our own beliefs and biases regarding the information we are now privy to in the process of historical inquiry. Probably the greatest question students of history must ask themselves when they reach an uncomfortable and unwelcome realization is "What do I do with this now?" This quandary reminds me of a line from T. S. Eliot's poem *The Waste Land*: "After such knowledge, what forgiveness?"[14] From this vantage point, once a new way of looking at the past has been imparted, there is no possibility (save for an amnesiac episode) of forgetting, much less unlearning, what has been discovered by or disclosed to those of us who study the past. Consequently, in addition to a sense of memory, critical reasoning, curiosity, and diligence, persons who commit themselves to the study of history have to have a great deal of resolve. This particular trait is necessary especially when the queries being asked and answered challenge core beliefs and expose aspects of one's own faith and traditions to scrutiny. In these moments of extreme self-consciousness and unease, it is that sense of resolve that coincides with the other aforementioned attributes that allow the historian to approach the work with the ironclad commitment to follow the trail of evidence wherever it may lead. Contemporary life forces us to live such conflicting loyalties that we must consciously resolve to cultivate a hermeneutic that allows us to stare directly into the heart of the belief systems and faith communities we are investigating in an unflinching manner, even if they are our own.

This book is about bearing witness to the story of a liberating faith in action in three broad streams. In this spirit, it is divided into three chapters. Chapter 1 narrates the transformation of Black faith and culture in the North American context from enslavement to emancipation; bar none, the signature feature of this era was the realization of freedom. Next, chapter 2 will deal with Black people's confrontation with the crisis of segregation and how it led to the culmination of the civil rights struggle in the United States and beyond; undeniably, the emphasis of this era focused most intently upon the establishment of justice for each member of American society. Finally, chapter 3 focuses on the contemporary developments in the religious experience of African Americans as they moved from the Black Power era to the age of Barack Obama; in the final analysis, this era is defined by the advancement of greater levels of equality for all people. These chapters share the lessons the dark past has taught me: that the history of Black people's religious quest for liberation has been a long but intermittent struggle for freedom, justice, and equality in this nation.

chapter 1

WAKING THE NATIONS UNDERGROUND

The Black Church Tradition from Enslavement to Emancipation

You'll hear the trumpet sound
to wake the nations underground
looking to God's right hand
when the stars began to fall

Traditional spiritual, "My Lord, What a Morning"

Anyone familiar with the slave spiritual "My Lord, What a Morning" might know that the song's title has been called alternately "morning" and "mourning." In describing this particular spiritual, musicologist John Lovell Jr.'s masterwork, *Black Song: The Forge and the Flame*, says that using the term *mourning* as a homophone for *morning* was a marker of the complex reality experienced by enslaved Africans and their American descendants. They used it to express both "the beginning of a great day of justice, accompanied by falling stars, moaning sinners, thundering trumpets, nations waking underground, and of course shouting Christians gliding toward heav'm [*sic*]."[1] In its call to "wake the nations underground," the song boldly alerts everyone—not only the living but also the dead and as-yet-unborn—about the imminent arrival of God's eternal justice in the earthly and heavenly realms. Embedded within the dual image of "mourning" and "morning" at the

21

heart of this song is the bittersweet quality of the sacred Black musical tradition that historian W. E. B. DuBois dubbed the "sorrow songs." Recognizing the critical insights and creative genius of spirituals such as this, DuBois contends that the spirituals "are the articulate message of the slave to the world. . . . They are the music of an unhappy people, of the children of disappointment; they tell of death and suffering and unvoiced longing toward a truer world, of misty wanderings and hidden ways."[2]

In a similar vein, this chapter utilizes this duality to illustrate both the horrible and hopeful dimensions of African American religious faith from its inception to emancipation. This faith took shape long before Africans landed on American shores, a perspective that is often eschewed in historical treatments of Black women, men, and children's progression from enslavement to emancipation. The signature feature of this era was the realization of freedom. Moreover, whereas the "nations underground" invoked in the song's lyrics could easily be considered the deceased being raised from the dead on the day of final judgment, the interpretation that comes to mind by talk of the morning suggests the awakening of the spiritual power of all African ancestors—the living, the dead, and the as yet unborn—on both sides of the Atlantic Ocean through a reclamation of our cultural heritage and sacred worldview as our undeniable birthright. Therefore, "waking the nations underground" asserts that writing a history of Black faith in our present moment is very much a process of reuniting and reawakening contemporary generations of readers (most particularly those of African descent) to their own hidden histories before, during, and after slavery, so that they can chart a clear course forward through the murky haze of the past.

BLACK RELIGION AND THE MIDDLE PASSAGE

To understand the history of Black religion in America, it is important to return to its origins. For all intents and purposes, the Black Church arose from the deepest, darkest depths of the slave ship. As millions of enslaved Africans were forced to travel across the Atlantic Ocean during the Middle Passage, aboard vessels ironically named *King of Dahomey, Brotherhood, The Virgin Mary,* and *John the Baptist,* their fervent prayers and pleas to the Almighty Creator marked the start of a radically different religious enterprise in the New World. As historian Charles Long asserts,

> The Middle Passage . . . was never forgotten by the Africans, neither during slavery nor in freedom. The watery passage of the Atlantic, that fearsome journey, that cataclysm of modernity, has served as a mnemonic structure, evoking a memory that forms the disjunctive and involuntary presence of these Africans in the Atlantic world.[3]

From the bowels of those dreaded wooden ships, untold millions of African women, men, and children began to shed many of the social, ethnic, and psychological distinctions that had kept them divided in their native lands on the continent.[4] In the hull of any given slave ship, en route to the most dehumanizing and devastating form of enslavement known to humankind, millions of Africa's children turned their souls to an unknown, unnamed God who might hold the answer to their present fate.

For the women, men, and children brought to the New World in the holds of slave ships, religion was a central, albeit contested, reality for those Africans and their offspring. Although some of the captives had been introduced to various expressions of religion—particularly Christianity—long before the arrival of European slave traders, the development of the Middle Passage did foment a crisis of faith for the enslaved. Vincent Harding describes this predicament in heart-wrenching terms:

> This ambivalence is not new. It was ours from the beginning. For we first met the American Christ on slave ships. We heard his name sung in hymns of praise while we died in our thousands, chained in stinking holds beneath the decks, locked in with terror and disease and sad memories of our families and homes. When we leaped from the decks to be seized by sharks we saw his name carved on the ships' solid sides. When our women were raped in the cabins they must have noticed the great and holy books on the shelves.[5]

As Harding suggests, viewing the Middle Passage as the first encounter of enslaved Africans with American Christianity is deeply problematic in nature. In the process of dehumanizing Black people en route to an uncertain fate, slave traders and slave masters were motivated to introduce Christianity to African captives, not for Christian charity or benevolence but rather to indoctrinate them into subservient obedience. Nevertheless, as Africans underwent what Albert Raboteau refers to as the "death of the gods," their collective encounter with Christianity helped galvanize their desperate agony into a new level of faith and spirituality.[6]

Early African American religion was an effort by enslaved Africans to safeguard themselves against the disruption of their religious worldview. Enslaved Africans gradually merged their composite African religiosity with Western notions of Christianity through complex cultural processes of enculturation, adaptation, and assimilation.[7] Whether enslaved or free, African American converts to Christianity in colonial America subordinated European sacred rhetoric and symbols to their own hermeneutical interpretation of personal salvation, conviction of sin, charismatic praise and worship, the equality of all peoples, and the divine promise of heaven.

No matter how distinctive and uniquely identifiable it might be, the Black Church tradition shares deeply significant connections with the other spiritual traditions held dear by people of African descent. Much like the other religions of the African diaspora, the Black Church tradition clearly has its roots in Central and West African cosmological systems that migrated along with women, men, and children of African descent as they made their captive passage across the Atlantic Ocean headed for the New World.[8] Much like its analogous faith traditions within the African diaspora, the Black Church tradition derived much of its unique heritage in terms of beliefs, values, and rituals from a seemingly discordant array of African, European, Native American, and countless other sources. Nevertheless, one definitive aspect of African American Christianity as it has been passed down to successive generations has been its special emphasis on the believers' collective spiritual rootedness to their African ancestry, however broadly conceived or narrowly construed.

Despite however many great differences that are manifest in their respective recognition and celebration of that spirituality, each African diasporan tradition—including African American Christianity—lays claim to this common inheritance. In his consideration of the significance of the longevity of cultural practices within the African diaspora, poet and cultural critic Amiri Baraka contends that

> music, dance, religion, do not have artifacts as their end products so they were saved. These nonmaterial aspects of the African culture were impossible to eradicate. And these are the most apparent legacies of the African past, even to the contemporary Black American blues, jazz, and the adaptation of the Christian religion, all rely heavily on African culture.[9]

Arguably, the diversity of worldviews and worship styles of the various African diasporan traditions can be understood by tracing the separate paths of historical development they undertook in the slave and post-emancipation societies of the Western Hemisphere. For instance, Haiti declared itself a free and independent Black republic and ended slavery in 1804. Although abolition of slavery in Jamaica officially took place in 1834, the island remained a British colony until 1962. In the American South during the antebellum era, freed Black people were a miniscule fraction of the overall population, whereas roughly a third of the Black inhabitants in pre-abolition Cuba were free. Home to the most people of African descent outside the African continent, Brazil did not outlaw the peculiar institution of slavery until 1888, making it the last New World society to do so. Using this brief historical comparison, one can get a glimpse at how each African-derived spiritual tradition developed its own unique expression in light of the varied challenges each faced in terms of geographical and historical context. Thus we have Vodoun in Haiti, Obeah in Jamaica, African American Christianity in the United States, Santería in Cuba, and Candomblé in Brazil, among a host of others. Each of these African diasporan traditions shares a common history of enslavement, disenfranchisement, exploitation, and dehumanization in the New World. Yet for the faithful adherents of these traditions, each belief system also served as a sacred site where they could engage in an extraordinary struggle for survival and ultimate victory over the brutality of inhuman bondage in its myriad forms. Moreover, although divided by geography, language, and political system, these traditions are linked by a heightened sense of solidarity against injustice and preservation predicated upon their embrace of the spirit.

Having said all that, the study of African American religious history has much work to do in order to balance and integrate our appreciation for the diverse religious traditions within the African diaspora. Much like the spirit that invigorates and guides them, these traditions are many, and yet they are one simultaneously. However, within the historiography of African American religion, there have been typically two dialectical modes of analysis at work in examining Black religious traditions. The first dialectic focuses on similarities of Black Protestant denominations to one another in contradistinction to the white mainline Christianity of Europe and North America, using race as the primary source of identity and distinction. The second dialectic juxtaposes the beliefs, practices, and institutions of Black religious believers within a given religious community to another (i.e., assessing Black Pentecostal churches in comparison to their Black Baptist and Methodist counterparts), essentially using religious denomination or doctrine as the line of demarcation. Much less common is a historical purview that actually holds the Black Christian experience in tandem rather than in tension with the other religions of the African diaspora, both Christian and non-Christian alike.

To refine this point even further, this expanded outlook would also require looking at both the Black Church tradition and other African-derived religious traditions in new ways. On the one hand, thinking about the Black Church tradition would have to relinquish some of the acceptance of American exceptionalism that has been informed partially by an inherently Eurocentric Christian theology that arose over the last five centuries. Doing so would thus entail envisioning the members and institutions of the Black Church tradition in modes of comparison, competition, and even conversation with the Other in their own midst (whether this reflects people of different faith backgrounds, nationalities, sexual orientations, political ideologies, and so on). On the other hand, looking at the religions of the African diaspora in more meaningful ways would dictate understanding that they are recognized as historical and theological contemporaries rather than monolithic artifacts frozen in time and space. First, while they are similar, all African-derived faith traditions are not identical or interchangeable. When we look at the African continent, the varieties of indigenous communities and traditions—whether we talk about the Yoruba, Wolof, Akan, Mande, Ibo, or Fon peoples—are as distinct and specific in their respective spiritual beliefs and practices from one another as they are from the Black religions scattered across the Black Atlantic. Similarly, just because we talk about Haitian Vodoun, Cuban Santería, or Jamaican Obeah as religions "from the islands" (in other words, having Afro-Caribbean origins) in reductionist, overly generalized terms denies the fact that these traditions are profoundly different in terms of vitality, diversity, and internal dynamics.

Additionally, in discussing the religions of Africa and the diaspora, we should also be mindful of addressing these traditions in contemporaneous as well as in historical terms. For instance, according to recent estimates, there will be an estimated five hundred million—yes, a half billion—Africans who self-identify as Christian by the year 2030, far exceeding the anticipated growth of the church in Europe and the United States.[10] Not only does this represent a demographic that is roughly 1.5 times the current size of the entire US population, it also reflects a mode of modern Christianity that is not on the decline as is visible in Europe. Moreover, with its dizzying mélange of religions ranging from the most traditional to the most modern, how the African continent deals with its wealth of spiritual diversity moving into the future might serve as an exemplar on issues of religious pluralism and interreligious dialogue for decades to come. However, such lessons can never be gleaned if our attempts to describe Africa and Africans perpetually render them as the land and people that time has forgotten.

Over the long haul, the study of change and continuity within the Black Church tradition paradoxically has much to learn from the heterogeneity and adaptability that formed the Black religious experience in it earliest moments from Africa to America. In an effort to embrace new ways of looking at African American religion, there is a need to go back to its roots. This point suggests that we must examine and scrutinize long-standing assumptions and conventional views of the Black Church tradition in light of critical insights and new scholarship, with a keen eye both to its contemporary utility and future effectiveness.

This process of assessing the present and of rethinking long-held assumptions about faith involves looking both backward and forward. At times like this, students of history need to reflect on what churches and other faith communities are currently doing but also look back to the formative eras of the past. At the start of this century, historical research is committed to taking a fresh look at the complexity of the periods from ancestors all over what Paul Gilroy has dubbed the "Black Atlantic." Even though we academics like to imagine ourselves as open-minded and forward-looking, there is an aversion to envisioning change within the Black Church tradition. In a context in which so much seems to be either uncertain or set adrift in so many ways, the ways we view the Black Church tradition, the basis of our worldview and source of our faith, is expected to remain static.[11]

When considered seriously, based on the etymological roots of the term *religion* derived from two Latin words, *re* and *ligare*, meaning "to bind again," we can imagine the religious dimension of the African diaspora that actually represents a scattering and reconnecting of self to both the Divine as well as the world. Through the process of reliving, renewing, and re-creating faithful practices, customs, and beliefs, there is a perpetual process of remembrance, reconciliation, and reunion at work in that quintessential human need to either adapt or die. The history of African American religion is replete with stories of ancestors throughout various eras who have attempted to preserve cultural integrity and spiritual resolve in various moments of crisis by going back to fundamental sources. Nevertheless sincere questions about the Black Church tradition and the possibility of change still persist. While it is abundantly clear that the Black Church tradition is not an endangered species in terms of tradition *per se* (it has been around for a long time), we must seriously respect that tradition as a central concern is different from traditionalism.

What comes to mind when we think of traditions? Tradition can be defined as the passing of beliefs, values, knowledge, and actions from one generation to the next through oral rather than written instruction.[12] Additionally, each particular group recognizes tradition as an inherited or established pattern of thought, being, or deed that has consistent and sustained usage over time. Most germane to our discussion here, religious tradition is construed as the process of continuity in moral attitudes, social institutions, and cultural norms.[13] When thinking about religious matters, we all participate in the carrying and handling of tradition as we experience and express our spiritual selves. We are all actively involved in the process of making tradition not as a static entity but as a living enterprise. What we should fear and avoid is the propensity to lapse into traditionalism as a means of capturing the story of Black faith in a veritable freeze-frame.

Whether discussing the interpretive process in the study of religion and theology or the liturgical and ecclesial life of churches, there must be an active, almost willful, effort to move beyond the question, "Can anything true come from something new?" In so doing, historians can engage in the interplay of tradition and traditions that make it possible to listen and learn from those voices that have been ignored, marginalized, or silenced by the stifling force of traditionalism. In his classic study of slave religion in North America, Albert Raboteau focuses on the divergence between the theologies of Black Protestantism in the United States and African diasporan traditions such as Vodoun, Santería, and Candomblé:

> While there may be similar effects—ego enhancement and catharsis, to name only two—on this level of faith event, there are major differences between spirit possession as it occurs in African and Latin American cults, on the one hand, and the ecstatic shouting experience of United States revivalism on the other. . . . The African gods with their myriad characteristics, personalities, and myths do not "mount" their enthusiasts amid the dances, songs and drum rhythms of worship in the United States. Instead it is the Holy Spirit who fills the converted sinner with a happiness and power that drives him [or her] to shout, sing, and sometimes dance.[14]

In this and other examples, Raboteau considers this phenomenon a representation of what he calls the "death of the gods," a process for enslaved Africans and their descendants in North America that led to the rise of "slave religion" and its gradual evolution into African American

Christianity. In so doing, he greatly mitigates the claims of scholars who boldly contend that there is a relatively seamless continuation of African cultural traits within African American traditions in modern life.[15] Nevertheless, this begs the question: Can a god truly die? For the many millions of Black women, men, and children who were trapped within the Transatlantic Slave Trade, their belief in a spirit that animates us and brought all life into existence was still present and seeking expression. Therefore, although imbued with the sort of cataclysmic trauma indicative of what Orlando Patterson refers to as "social death," Raboteau's argument about the ontological shift from an exclusively African spirituality toward the hybrid African American Christianity is still marked by the oppressive and abusive elements amassed against Black believers. For instance, there is an implicit notion within the work of Raboteau and others that pre-colonial West African deities and sacred beliefs were unfit for the New World so the "death of the gods" in favor of Christianity was inevitable. Such a fate, however, was not an absolute or automatic fact of Black religious life in the Americas at the height of the Transatlantic Slave Trade.

A work that builds upon Raboteau's "death of the gods" thesis but also advances it in provocative ways is Michael A. Gomez's recent work in analyzing the cultural transformation of African ethnicities into a composite African American identity. While Gomez is clearly mindful of the legacy of horror and brutally wrought by the Middle Passage and the subsequent enslavement of African peoples in the Americas, his work suggests that these kidnapped and displaced people invariably held on to their core culture much longer than previously imagined. In some cases they steadily handed down elements of their original African ethnicity to following generations in an uninterrupted manner. In recognizing that Black women, men, and children might bear the spiritual as well as physical characteristics of their African ancestry well beyond the trials and travails of chattel slavery, Gomez notes a key factor in this process of cultural hybridization: agency. By noting levels of resistance and resilience within African-derived cultures in the Americas, Gomez's perspective challenges Raboteau's original thesis and, by so doing, suggests that maybe the gods of Africa received a new lease on life as well.[16]

As an earlier interpreter of African cultural retention and hybridity, Melville J. Herskovits argues the similarities of sacred rituals and worldviews within the African diaspora quite forcefully when he writes:

> Stress is laid on the outer forms of religious expression rather than on inner values and beliefs. For, as will be seen, while Christian doctrine by no means escaped change as it passed into Negro hands, the most striking and recognizable survivals of African religion are in those behavioristic aspects that, given overt expression, are susceptible of reinterpretation in terms of a new theology while retaining their older established forms [*sic*].[17]

Whereas the varieties of religious traditions within the African diaspora should not be overemphasized—particularly in the experiential dimension—such traits should be neither diminished nor ignored.

More often than not, this process of cultural hybridity and reinvention within the Black religious experience is most evident in association with funerals. As I have attended more than my fair share of "homegoing" services, it is a remarkable act to witness these pivotal events from a historian's perspective. Although it might seem morbid, death often invokes the need for historical inquiry, a need to make sense of a life that has been lived. Danish philosopher and theologian Søren Kierkegaard states the situation this way: "Life can only be understood backwards; but it must be lived forwards."[18] As family members, friends, acquaintances, and onlookers gather to celebrate a life that has made the ultimate transition, each person wrestles with and often recounts episodes culled from their experiences with the dearly departed in distinctly different ways according to their own perspectives. The thought that young folks might be listening to grown-ups as they exchange tales about the fuller story of the deceased person's life and times is a remarkable occurrence. As such, funeral rituals are not only a means of commemorating those who passed away but also a sort of collective biography wherein we write aloud an important part of personal and family history in addition to passing it on to the next generation.

The way that African peoples face mortality illuminates the unique and profound primacy of death within the African worldview and subsequently the African American experience. Even at the time of this writing, thoughts on the terror attacks of September 11, 2001; the ongoing repercussions of the Afghanistan and Iraq wars; and cataclysmic natural disasters such as Hurricane Katrina, the 2010 Haitian earthquake, and Superstorm Sandy have drastically altered many people's consciousness about human mortality. When discussing the ways in which African Americans grappled with the cultural, historical, and spiritual resonance of death on their collective psyches, historian W. E. B. DuBois wrote, "Of death the Negro showed little fear, but talked of it familiarly and even fondly as simply crossing the waters, perhaps—who knows?—back to [his or her] ancient forests again."[19] For instance, from the start of the Transatlantic Slave Trade through the decline of chattel slavery during the Civil War, the prospect of death was repeatedly imagined by the enslaved as a strange sort of freedom—the ultimate "sweet release"—from an unbearable life of tyranny and oppression. When enslaved Africans were initially brought to the New World as captive cargo, many believed wholeheartedly that the spirits of the deceased would make the journey back to their native land.

In many regards, this suggests the extent to which the whole notion of "homegoing" as a process of the deceased shedding the physical burdens of the world and having their spiritual essence transcend the harrowing misery and despair of this mortal realm was a matter of celebration rather than dread within the African American cultural imagination. Although always acknowledging the sacredness of life as a much-revered gift from God, these forebears also bore witness to the fact that death signified a means of utter and absolute emancipation from the pains of an existence plagued with unyielding oppression and inhumane abuse. This sensibility is most stunningly captured in the words of the well-known slave spiritual "Oh, Freedom," which declares: "And before I'll be a slave / I'd be buried in my grave / And go home to my Lord / And be free." Mourners engaged in slave burials reportedly sang other spirituals such as "Lay Dis Body Down," "Hark from de Tomb, a Doleful Sound," and "Deep River" during the rituals.

When looking at the embedded theology within the spirituals, "Deep River" is noteworthy for its lyrics: "Deep River, my home is over Jordan, / Deep river, Lord; I want to cross over into camp ground." While a literal interpretation of this song's lyrics indicates the African

American religious belief that a person's soul journeyed across the River Jordan upon death, this also evoked the West African belief that water connected the realms of the living and the dead. Articulating a vision of death that welcomes the spiritual transition to the afterlife while also denouncing the grave injustice marked by enslavement, these people defiantly expressed the radical spirit of freedom in their full appreciation of homegoing as a part of God's providential plan of liberation. When viewed in this light, we see that matters of death and dying have been intertwined with the desire for life and liberty in extremely complex ways both during and after slavery.[20]

Without question, the integral relationship of death and dying can be traced back to cosmological views and traditional customs prevalent within pre-colonial West and Central Africa. The inescapable centrality of the funeral among the peoples of the African diaspora arose from deeply held beliefs that the living, deceased, and not-yet-born all existed within this earthly realm under the provenance of the Supreme Creator. As such, the dead and living are never fully separated from one another in a strictly binary fashion; but instead they are always immediately and intimately interconnected.[21]

Unlike the concept of death as the irrevocable loss of the dearly departed by the living survivors that pervades Western European religious beliefs, traditional African cosmologies have perennially envisioned the newly dead uniting with deceased ancestors to serve as dynamic spiritual guides who influence and protect the living in meaningful ways. Even though the ethnic and religious diversity present on the African continent makes it quite difficult to make claims about views on death and funeral rituals that are absolutely irrefutable, it is feasible to discuss the general principles of West and Central African religious beliefs and ritual praxis related to death in the hopes of demonstrating how they have helped inform the African American cultural imagination about death and dying over time.

Over five hundred years ago, these funerary rituals migrated across the Black Atlantic as a result of the Middle Passage to find a home in the Americas. In wrestling with the inevitability of human fatality, traditions surrounding African burial practices and bereavement rituals soon influenced how American-born descendants of enslaved

33

Africans developed slave funerals from the colonial era to the antebellum era. The overwhelming majority of enslaved African women, men, and children who were brought to North America hailed from the Congo-Angola region of Central Africa's western coast. For the Bakongo people of West Africa, their traditional religious beliefs embraced the concept of a two-tiered realm of existence divided quite simply between "this world" and "the other world." On the one hand, "this world" belonged to the living, wherein they experienced all the tragedies and triumphs of life in between the moment of birth and death. On the other hand, "the other world" belonged to the ancestors, the not-yet-born, ghosts, and all manner of spirits who could exert their supernatural power upon the affairs of the living in unforeseen ways. In an interesting tribute to the deceased, the Bakongo made a ritual practice of planting trees on or near gravesites so that, as the tree's roots grew downward, they illustrated the soul's journey to the other world.[22] These and other burial practices reflect how West African traditional religions in general and Kongo cosmology in particular fully embraced a dynamic synergy that existed between the spirits of the deceased and the living.

Viewed in this fashion, death was not perceived as a bitter and fateful end; but instead it was merely considered as a transition to another phase of the human life cycle. For that reason, preparing and burying the dead was treated as an elaborate set of rituals and processes intended to fully honor the spirit of the deceased, as well as properly guide their spiritual essence toward its new home in the other world. Within this cosmological belief, as historian Suzanne Smith argues, "The profound cultural significance of the funeral in African society, and subsequently in African American life, arose from the basic but essential belief that one's deceased ancestors have direct relationship with and authority over the lives of their descendants."[23] To make this point perfectly clear, it is understood within such a worldview of ancestral veneration that the deceased are no longer "alive" in literal terms. Rather, they are acknowledged as extremely powerful spiritual forces who can influence and intercede on behalf of their descendants and loved ones in the realm of the living. In his landmark text, *The Myth of the Negro Past*, anthropologist Melville Herskovits writes, "The dead are everywhere regarded as close to the forces that govern the universe, and are believed to influence the well-being of their descendants who properly serve them."[24] Understood in this fashion, the African American relationship to death begins to make more sense as a matter of both historical and spiritual importance. What makes the transference and retention of African folkways about death and burial so remarkable is that, unlike the wide range of funerary practices in many other global cultures, the persistence of these death practices with African American culture had to "survive" the devastation of capture, the Middle Passage, and New World enslavement in order to enable African Americans to use West African rituals and beliefs in order to meet their own needs in other parts of the African diaspora.[25]

Generally, West and Central Africans place the utmost importance on burial among one's clan in their home village, even going so far as contributing money on a communal basis in order to transport the body home if the deceased should die far from home. As a merger of material and spiritual concerns, financial hardship during a funeral is never a consideration. As such, the funeral tradition ranks as the highest of all social practices wherein it functions as a cohesive force within the community. Such funeral practices exist in Ghana, Sierra Leone, Nigeria, Benin, Liberia, Congo, Angola, and Cameroon. Central features of the funeral traditions include dancing, drumming, and feasting. But these elaborate funeral rites are notable for a host of other reasons as well. For instance, the ceremonial use of umbrellas in Nigeria represents a person's wealth and social status. In Benin and Ghana, funerals operate as a "farewell party" for the deceased with farce and humor as modes of entertainment and celebration for the living and the dead alike. All told, across these cultures, the funeral serves as a sophisticated occasion for demarcating the social status among the dead, as a means of escorting the dead into the afterlife and as a means of reinforcing communal responsibility for all matters pertaining to the funeral.

Beginning with West and Central African traditions, we shall move briefly to the African American experience with death and dying in the North American context. When considering the African American funeral tradition, the narrative of race and racism is virtually inescapable. In her study on African Americans' encounters with death and bereavement, literary scholar Karla Holloway illustrates how the segregated nature of Black funerals made them exceptional events on the American scene due to the dichotomous nature of Black and white funerals.[26] Naming the Black Church tradition and its funerary rites as "articulating the shape of black culture," their corporate ritual "encouraged a necessary cultural dialectic between sacred aspiration and secular experience."[27] Holloway describes fundamental differences between Black and white experiences with mourning as consisting primarily of the emotive dimension, which serves as a catharsis for the sorrows of this world, a release—no matter how temporary—from suffering and a place for mourning what Holloway calls "black death" (death from racially determined causes). Additionally, Holloway also points out several African retentions, in particular the call-and-response style of African American worship that consequently has had implications for African American performance of all types.[28] Most notably, Holloway observes that African American funeral customs match the cultural pattern of mourning, procession, and celebration evident in West African societies.[29] Food and feasting is central to the mourning process both before and after the burial of the deceased. Holloway also mentions that, on occasions, in lieu of a local church, social clubs, and funeral associations, African Americans offered visitations and "settin'-ups" (events comparable to wakes or vigils) for the bereaved.[30] In the antebellum era, white slaveholders did not always allow the burial services of enslaved Blacks. Even when slave masters finally did allow funeral services to occur, the burials were often limited to one night or possibly the day after but never any longer than that. Therefore, the mandates of the slave masters invariably violated the typical three-day duration of the West African funeral practice. Consciously or not, this measure effectively forced the Black celebrants to compress the whole range of funeral-related activities out of sheer necessity.

THE SLAVE CODES AND THE EMERGENCE OF BLACK RELIGION

When slavery was introduced to the English colony of Jamestown in 1619, there was no official distinction of "slave" in English law. By the end of the seventeenth century, however, this fact changed with a series of influential legal measures approved by the Virginia House of Burgesses known as the Slave Codes. These codes profoundly defined race relations in North America more than a century before the ratification of the US Constitution. By 1650, Virginia legislators established the premise that Africans were considered enslaved for life as a *de facto* (by custom) issue. A noteworthy 1662 law emphasized children of an enslaved or indentured mother inherited the legal status of their mother in clear violation of English common law and custom. Another 1662 law stated that "if any *Christian* shall [commit] Fornication with a negro man or woman, hee or shee [*sic*] so offending" would be doubly fined as opposed to those found guilty of a similar offense between two "Christians." By 1667, the House of Burgesses passed a law that Christian baptism no longer allowed for the liberation of enslaved peoples. In 1670 the Virginia legislature ratified a law that any non-Christian servants brought by ship "shall be slaves for their lives"; this mandated that slavery was *durante vita* (for life) and *de jure* (by law). By 1705, legislation was passed that enslaved labor was to be considered chattel (private property).[31]

With the ascendancy of chattel slavery in American life, the most significant examination of modern language coincides with the decision to use of the term *enslaved Africans*, instead of the more common word *slave*. Aside from any claims of political correctness, the scrupulous use of the modifier enslaved serves at least two purposes. First, the way we use language such as enslaved versus slave to describe historical Black persons and communities is an outright attempt to redeem the humanity of those women, men, and children of African descent. Second and more important, the choice of vernacular is to remind the writer and reader alike that the condition of bondage in which these persons found themselves did not exclusively define or exhaust the depth of their humanity. This adds poignancy because the witness of so many Black Christians in bondage was that even though their material state was one of enslavement, they nevertheless strove to realize a spiritual and mental state of freedom.

The legal evolution of chattel slavery is further complicated by the fact that when Black women were brought from Africa to the New

World as enslaved laborers, their value was determined by their ability to work as well as their potential to bear children, who by law would become the enslaved property of the mother's master. In her recent work, historian Jennifer L. Morgan examines how African women's labor—in both senses— became indispensable in the English colonies. By challenging conventional logic, Morgan reveals how expectations regarding gender and reproduction were central to racial ideologies, the organization of slave labor, and fomenting notions of community and even resistance amongst the enslaved. Taking into consideration the heritage of Africans prior to enslavement and the cultural logic of values and practices recreated under the duress of slavery, she examines how women's gender identity was defined by their conjoined experiences as both agricultural laborers and mothers. By and large, this distinction shows how their situation differed considerably from that of enslaved men. Moving along the arc of enslaved African women's actual lives—from West Africa, to the experience of the Middle Passage, to life on the plantations—Morgan's research is invaluable in the ways it illustrates how Black women's reproductive experience shaped their roles in communities and also helped them resist some of the more egregious effects of inhuman bondage.[32]

Once enslaved Blacks were denied fellowship within the Christian churches of their era, they created what Albert Raboteau called "slave religion." The emergence of these new expressions of Black faith took shape through a process known as syncretism.[33] Slave religion is important to the origins of the Black Christian experience in America for two distinct reasons. On the one hand, retention of African traditional religions in the Western Hemisphere is evident in the persistence of such religious practices as spirit possession, river baptisms (total immersion), the ring shout, and call-and-response. Conjuring practices and cross-cultural identification of African divine spirits with Roman Catholic saints also became evident in African-derived religious traditions such as Santería from Cuba, Candomblé from Brazil, and Vodoun from Haiti.[34] On the other hand, it laid a religious foundation for the historic Black Church, whereby the spiritual and cultural sensibilities of enslaved Africans found common ground with various icons, rituals, and traditions within Western Christianity, which otherwise might not have been recognized. In this fashion, slave religion soon became the means to galvanize people of African descent into a more cohesive community based on their religious practices as well as their race.

RACE, SLAVERY, AND THE GREAT AWAKENINGS

The major turning point in African American Christianity and the creation of the historic Black Church tradition came in conjunction with periods of widespread pietism and religious revivalism known as the First and Second Great Awakenings. During the early 1730s, a Congregationalist preacher named Jonathan Edwards began a more emotional, participatory ministry aimed at bringing more people into the faith through baptism and conversion. By the 1740s, George Whitefield also carried an evangelical style of Christianity to the British colonies in North America. In their "fire and brimstone" sermons, Edwards and Whitefield—while they did not advocate emancipation—preached to Black people and white people alike.[35]

Some people of African descent had converted to Christianity before Whitefield's arrival in North America. But two factors prevented widespread Black conversion. First, most slave masters feared that enslaved Blacks who embraced Christianity would interpret their new religious status as a step toward freedom, justice, and equality. A South Carolina minister lamented in 1713, "The Masters of Slaves are generally of Opinion that a Slave grows worse by being a Christian; and therefore instead of instructing them in the principles of Christianity . . . malign and traduce those that attempt it."[36] Second, many enslaved Blacks continued to derive spiritual satisfaction from their ancestral religions and were not attracted to the Christianity of European settlers.

With the First Great Awakening, however, a remarkable conversion began along cultural and spiritual lines. Enslaved Africans, and eventually their African American counterparts, now not only became Christians but also, in turn, influenced white religiosity. This was because this religious movement unwittingly emphasized key points of convergence between Western Christianity and African traditional religions. For instance, the prevalent belief in a supreme being, ancestral veneration, and animism within African traditional religions resembled the trinitarian belief in the "Father, Son, and Holy Ghost" central to mainstream Christian doctrine. Moreover, the revivalist style of preaching adopted by Whitefield and other evangelicals had some overt similarities to forms of "spirit possession" that were commonplace in West African societies. Like their African and African American counterparts—both enslaved and free—white evangelists and revivalists of the First Great Awakening emphasized singing, emotionalism, physical movement, and personal rebirth. The practice of total body immersion during baptism in lakes, rivers, and ponds that gave the Baptist church its name paralleled the West African water rituals.

Although it was impossible to avoid some degree of cross-fertilization between African American Christianity and the white mainline Protestant church, the very existence of the Black Church tradition bespeaks the inability of Western Christianity to incorporate any mode of beliefs, praxis, and experiences largely because the mainline church defined itself in contradistinction to the reality of the enslaved.[37] Because it drew African Americans into an evangelical movement that helped shape American society, the First Great Awakening increased the infusion of Western Christianity into the Black religious experience. Revivalists appealed to the poor of all races and emphasized spiritual equality. Evangelical Anglicans, Baptists, Methodists, Congregationalists, and Presbyterians during the colonial era opened their fledgling churches to Black people. Members of these early interracial churches addressed each as "brother" and "sister" regardless of race. Black members received communion with white members, served as church officers, and were subject to the same church discipline.

By the late 1700s, Black men such as Jupiter Hammon, David George, George Liele, and Andrew Bryan were being ordained as deacons, priests, exhorters, and ministers—even though they were enslaved—and they preached to white congregations. They thereby influenced white people's perception of how services should be conducted. Black worshipers also influenced white preachers. In 1756, a white minister in Virginia noted that African Americans spent nights in his kitchen. He recorded in his diary that "sometimes, when I have awakened about two or three a-clock in the morning, a torrent of sacred harmony poured into my chamber, and carried my mind away to Heaven."[38] Regardless of race, the Baptists and Methodists exhibited a worship style that was revival-minded and enthusiastic; this, however, had a particular impact on African Americans who resonated with a form of Christianity that was reminiscent of African traditional religions.

One must recall that during the mid- to late 1700s, in which the First Great Awakening occurred, there were divergent perspectives of how some white Christian groups were attempting to deal with the ramifications of Christian conversion in matters of race and slavery. For instance, there were two religious encounters with African Americans in northern American colonies. On the one hand, the Puritans (Congregationalists) of New England sought to convert Africans and yet maintain slavery so as to prevent economic losses and social upheaval. The white Congregationalists wanted minimal contact with Africans whether enslaved or free. On the other hand, the Quakers (Society of Friends) sought to convert Africans and end slavery. Their liberal mode of worship allowed for possibility of salvation for enslaved people and promoted equality. Emblematic of the Quaker leadership elite's moral fortitude during the revolutionary era, the Pennsylvania legislature banned chattel slavery in 1780.

Meanwhile, the Society for the Propagation of the Gospel in Foreign Parts operated under a significantly different agenda toward the Christianization of African Americans in southern American colonies. The Society for the Propagation of the Gospel in Foreign Parts was an Anglican organization that sought to convert Africans and did not oppose slavery. They did not want to destabilize the institution of plantation slavery or upset Southern planters who saw baptism of and teaching literacy to enslaved Africans and African Americans as threatening. As a result Southern planters had a very tenuous commitment to the mission of the Society for the Propagation of the Gospel in Foreign Parts.

During the First Great Awakening, enslaved preacher George Liele, the first Black Baptist preacher and missionary in Georgia, founded the Silver Bluff Baptist Church in Silver Bluff, South Carolina. This church is notable because it was a congregation that included free and enslaved Blacks. Andrew Bryan, one of Liele's original followers, along with support from several prominent white men of Savannah who cited the positive effect of religion on slave discipline, was ordained and his church certified in 1788. When his own master died, Andrew Bryan was able to purchase his freedom. In 1794, Bryan raised enough money to erect a church in Savannah, calling it the Bryan Street African Baptist Church—the first Baptist church for African Americans in Georgia (and probably the United States), as well as the first Baptist church, either Black or white, in Savannah. By 1800, the church had grown to about seven hundred; they reorganized as the First Baptist Church of Savannah, and 250 members were dismissed in order to establish a branch outside of Savannah.[39] The pioneering ministerial work of George Liele, David George, and Andrew Bryan boldly established the historic Afro-Protestant tradition within the African American religious experience.[40]

Enslaved Blacks found significant reasons to embrace the Baptist tradition in the antebellum South. Most separate Black Baptist congregations such as the Silver Bluff community (1770s) were typically southern and rural with notable exceptions like New York City's Abyssinian Baptist Church (1808). Even though there was a definite concept of the "call to ministry" for educated clergy and trained leadership within Baptist church doctrine, there was limited concern for educational qualifications regarding catechism and formal training. This was particularly advantageous for Black men and women who were forbidden access to any level of education by state law. Furthermore, the Baptists espoused the belief in the equality of all believers, with a great emphasis on moral self-determination—what historian Nathan Hatch has called the "individuation of conscience"—as well as independence and democratic order. Due to the congregational basis of Baptist churches, the decentralized autonomy of local communities of the faithful was vitally important for a fellowship of Black Christians who were forced, because of the virulent web of racial and religious persecution, to remain "invisible." This invisibility was further enhanced by the minimal supervision/monitoring of their worship services by white authorities. The general Baptist belief in human potential fulfilling God's will spoke intensely to an enslaved people who were continuously condemned as being subhuman by whites.

In a similar fashion, as a denomination based on connectional churches, the centralization of Methodist societies via regional meetings and conferences inherently led to a greater sense of church fellowship as well as a considerable pooling of resources. The accepted role of traveling or itinerant ministers proved less hierarchal than other denominations and also allowed for the opportunity for Black men and women to preach in various churches. Notable Methodist leaders such as John Wesley and Francis Asbury believed the gospel was meant for all people regardless of color; they argued that true Methodist societies must deny Christian fellowship to slaveholders. This level of antislavery advocacy was rare by any standard, and it had a definite allure for African Americans seeking a faith free of religious hypocrisy and moral contradiction.

For almost three years following the American Revolution, pioneering Black Methodist missionary and author John Marrant served as the pastor of a dedicated and growing congregation of Black Loyalists in Nova Scotia, who had emigrated there to escape chattel slavery in the American colonies. Having been sponsored by the Huntingdon Connection of Calvinist Methodists, Marrant upheld a Calvinist predestination doctrine rather than a Wesleyan theology of salvation, as he planted church starts among Africans and African Americans throughout the Atlantic world. Toward this end, he was devoted to spreading a mode of Christianity tailored to the specific social and political needs of Black women, men, and children. Marrant brought a "New Covenant." He used his autobiographical works and sermons to proclaim himself a prophet, and he supported efforts to migrate along with his congregation to Sierra Leone, where they intended to establish a free Black society as a new Zion. Marrant returned to London in March of 1790 to defend himself against charges of squandering his benefactor's contributions to his ministry. Ultimately, he would not live to see his congregation depart to settle in Sierra Leone in 1791 because he died that same year at the age of thirty-six.[41] Marrant's autobiographical writings document a life seemingly twice that length in experience in which he vigorously sought to build a new society worthy of salvation in the Nova Scotia wilderness around the Black Loyalists who fled there after the Revolutionary War.

By the end of the eighteenth century, along with the dawning of the American Republic in the wake of the Revolutionary War, independent

Black churches quickly became the core of African American communities. The roots of the independent Black Church movement are traced most often to the establishment of the Free African Society in Philadelphia in 1787. Richard Allen, Absalom Jones, and other African American members of St. George's Methodist Episcopal Church organized this church. The incident that led to the formation of the Free African Society was the forced removal of Absalom Jones from St. George's by the white trustees while he and other Black members were kneeling at the altar in prayer. Because of differences in religious views, Allen left the Free African Society in 1789, and Jones became its leader. Under Jones's leadership, the Free African Society began holding worship services on New Year's Day, 1791, and the society soon gave way to the formation of their own church. Over the next few years, Absalom Jones and the church's charter members petitioned the Episcopal Church to become an Episcopal parish yet fervently insisted upon remaining free of white control. As a result, Jones and the members founded St. Thomas African Episcopal Church in Philadelphia, thus making it the first independent Black church in Philadelphia. By 1805, Jones was ordained as the first African American Episcopalian priest in the nation.

Like Reverend Jones and Black Episcopalians, Richard Allen was vitally important to the formation of the independent Black Church movement. When the predominantly white congregation supported the racist actions of the trustees, Allen eventually organized his fellow Black Methodists in order to form the Bethel Church in 1793. Richard Allen was subsequently ordained by Methodist bishop Francis Asbury in 1799 and became the first Black Methodist minister. Realizing his great desire to build a house of worship for African Americans, Allen bought the land and built the sanctuary for Bethel Church in Philadelphia, which remains even now as the oldest continuously owned property by African Americans in this country. Richard Allen was elected its first bishop in 1816. Other African-identified churches in the area, having also been discriminated against by white Christians, aligned themselves with Bishop Allen, thus establishing the African Methodist Episcopal (AME) Church as the first Black Church denomination in the United States and with "Mother Bethel" AME Church as its flagship institution.[42] By 1848, Frederick Douglass maintained that the Mother

Bethel AME Church in Philadelphia, with its roughly three thousand worshipers every Sunday, was the "largest church in this Union."

The founding of the African Methodist Episcopal Zion Church (AME Zion) was another key example of the independent Black Church movement in America. The church's roots can be traced back to the John Street Methodist Church of New York City. Following acts of overt racial discrimination such as forcing Blacks to leave worship, many Black Methodists left to form their own churches. The first church founded by the AME Zion Church was built in 1800 and was henceforth named "Mother Zion." These early churches were still part of the Methodist Church, although the congregations remained separate. James Varick was elected in 1821 and ordained as the first bishop of the AME Zion Church a year later.[43] Early conflicts surfaced between the Allenites (supporters of Richard Allen) and Zionites (supporters of James Varick), particularly over territorial growth and expansion.

After 1816, the great enthusiasm among free Blacks surrounding the independent Black Church movement led to the burgeoning number of AME and AME Zion churches within cities in the northern and southern United States, thus establishing two new and distinctive Wesleyan denominations. Furthermore, the establishment of predominantly African United Baptist churches in Canada during the early half of the nineteenth century also offers signs of Black Christians' excitement over the creation of their own churches and denominations across national borders. On the whole, the independent Black Church movement was vital to the fabric of free Black communities in the North. The churches that were organized, supported, and led by Black Christians during the nineteenth century illustrated a sense of freedom in performing religious functions and guarding moral discipline and community values in addition to providing and promoting education, social insurance, fraternal associations, and recreation.[44]

During much of the Second Great Awakening, independent Black churches in the North were community centers in the truest sense. They housed schools and were meeting places for a variety of organizations as well as for various voluntary associations. Antislavery societies often met in churches, and the churches harbored fugitive slaves. This went hand-in-hand with the community leadership Black ministers provided to anxious church members who worried about the tenuous state of their quasi freedom. Black ministers had to regularly assuage their members while also keeping Black Northerners confident of God's grace and protection. The independent Black churches spoke against slavery in the plantation South as well as racial oppression in the North. These churches also grappled with what they considered to be weaknesses among African Americans. However, it must be noted that Black ministers seldom, if ever, spoke with a unanimous voice.

THE BLACK CHURCH AS THE "INVISIBLE INSTITUTION" IN THE OLD SOUTH

The free Black population doubled between 1820 and 1860 from 233,500 to more than 488,000 as a result of childbirth, successful escapes, purchasing freedom, and manumission. More than half of the free Blacks lived in the South, usually in the upper South (Virginia, West Virginia, Kentucky, Tennessee, and North Carolina), as they feared reenslavement in the Deep South (Alabama, Georgia, Louisiana, Mississippi, and South Carolina). They usually lived on impoverished rural farmlands; although they also lived in towns and cities. Typically limited in their employment opportunities, many free Blacks worked as farmhands, day laborers, or woodcutters in rural areas or in factories or at certain skilled jobs in nearby towns and cities. Once greater chances for work in skilled trades became more available to African Americans, jobs such as barbering, shoemaking, and plastering were reserved for Black men, while Black women worked as cooks, laundresses, and domestics. In some Southern cities such as New Orleans, Charleston, and Richmond, a small, mixed-race class of free Blacks emerged as an elite group closely connected to white society and removed from the mass of poor Blacks. A few even owned land and were themselves slave owners. The freed Black communities were generally older than the enslaved population, and many were mulattoes/Creole (biracial offspring with African and European heritage) or mestizos (multiracial offspring of African, European, and Native American ancestry). Like their free counterparts, enslaved Blacks sought freedom for themselves and their families through petitions to state legislatures, lawsuits against masters, direct pleas for emancipation in wills, purchasing their freedom, or running away.

Consequently, there were growing fears from whites regarding the growth of the free Black community in the antebellum era for a variety of reasons. White Southerners feared the influence of free Blacks on lower-class white workers and enslaved African Americans. Southern states designed a series of laws that specifically limited the mobility, rights, and opportunities of free Blacks. Usually, free Blacks could not vote, bear arms, buy liquor, assemble, speak in public, form societies, or testify against whites in court. There were organized attempts to confine free Blacks to certain areas of the city or force them to leave the city, county, or state altogether. By example, Texas won independence from Mexico in 1836 and promptly legalized slavery. During the establishment of the "Lone Star Republic," Texas created several laws in which free Blacks and Creoles were forbidden from entering the state. Those free Blacks who stayed in urban areas also had trouble finding work. They were required to carry licenses and "freedom papers" everywhere they traveled, and they often needed a white guardian to approve their actions. By the 1850s, the growing concern of white Southerners with the presence of free Blacks in their midst led to the threat of extinction for the free Black community.

By the nineteenth century, however, most African Americans in the antebellum South practiced a form of Protestantism that was loosely related to that of their white counterparts. Ironically, interracial Methodist and Baptist church fellowships persisted in the South much longer than they did in Northern cities. The Southern congregations usually had racially segregated seating, but free Blacks and whites joined in communion and congregational worship, and they even shared cemeteries in some locales.

Another aspect of this interracial Christianity was evident in that many plantation owners as well as white missionary organizations sponsored churches on Southern estates for the express purpose of indoctrinating enslaved men, women, and children during the antebellum era. In the plantation churches of the Old South, white ministers typically preached to their Black congregants that the Holy Bible taught that

47

Black people deserved to be subjugated as a result of the "Curse of Ham," and that "good slaves" must obey their earthly masters as they did God.[45] As it might be imagined, this was not what enslaved African Americans wanted to hear. In his ex-slave narratives, Cornelius Garner recalled "dat ole white preacher jest was telling us slaves to be good to our marsters. We ain't keer'd a bit 'bout dat stuff he was telling us 'cause we wanted to sing, pray, and serve God in our own way [*sic*]."[46] There is evidence that at times enslaved Blacks walked out on ministers who preached obedience from the pulpit.

Instead of attending and adhering to church services sponsored by slave masters, enslaved Blacks were able to create an "invisible institution," a secretive Black Church tradition, where they consecrated themselves for the purpose of resisting, escaping when possible, and ultimately surviving enslavement in the plantation South. Giving rise to the "hush harbors" (alternately referred to as "brush arbors"), the historic Black Church in the American South was defined by various factors. In the aftermath of slave rebellions and insurrection plots organized by enslaved Black preachers such as Gabriel Prosser, Denmark Vesey, and Nat Turner, the spread of religion among the enslaved Black population was deemed illegal by nearly all the state legislatures throughout the American South.[47] In light of this situation, these loose-knit congregations held secret meetings, led by enslaved Black men and women who were often formally uneducated yet called by God to proclaim the gospel.

Most notably, enslaved Blacks gathered together as a community within hush harbors during the period from the colonial era until the outbreak of the Civil War to perform slave funerals. Slave funerals were a crucial means that allowed enslaved Africans and their New World descendants to assert their divinely inspired sense of humanity and community. The lyrics of the traditional slave spiritual "Lay This Body Down" eloquently capture this scene:

I know moon-rise, I know star-rise,
Lay dis body down.
I walk in de moonlight, I walk in the starlight,
To lay dis body down.

I'll walk in de graveyard, I'll walk through the graveyard,
To lay dis body down . . . I go to de judgment in de evenin' of de day,
When I lay dis body down,
And my soul and your soul will meet in de day,
When I lay dis body down.

From their earliest inception, those clandestine funeral ceremonies served a threefold purpose. First, the slave funeral enabled the living to honor the deceased in such a manner that allowed the living to partake in ritual practices and expressions of their shared cultural heritage in order to reconnect spiritually with their former African homeland. Next, the slave funeral also enabled the enslaved Black women, men, and children to assert their own evolving religiosity with unparalleled levels of autonomy in the secluded privacy of the wooded enclaves beyond the confines of the plantation. Finally, the occurrence of the slave funeral within the hush harbor invariably tested the boundaries of the master-slave relationship because the enslaved community could reassert in an intensely meaningful ways the bonds of family, community, and human dignity, which the peculiar institution of slavery repeatedly stole from them.[48] It was only once the Black preacher officially preached the funeral sermon over the dead that the family and larger community could fully enjoy peace of mind in the knowledge that the spirit of the deceased was truly set free. Hence, the slave funeral served as the most vital training ground for the historic Black Church tradition.

Both the biblical references and teachings of these hush harbors, as well as slave rebellions plotted by Prosser, Vesey, and Turner among countless others, were largely centered on the Old Testament narrative of Exodus with its emphasis on God's deliverance of Moses and the Israelites from inhumane slavery. Finding immediate parallels between the Israelites' plight in Pharaoh's Egypt and the struggle of African Americans against American slavery, enslaved Black Christians preferred the lessons garnered from the exodus story to the consistent theology of Christian meekness, docile slaves, and divinely cursed Black people as professed by white supremacists.[49] Moreover, gathering together in wooded areas far from the prying eyes and relentless whips of those who enslaved them, Black Christians held worship services that were characterized by a sense of engaging ecstasy with singing, dancing, praying, moaning, clapping, and shouting.

The composers of Negro spirituals such as "Wade in the Water," "Swing Low, Sweet Chariot," and "Steal Away to Jesus" are unknown, but scholars such as W. E. B. DuBois, Howard Thurman, and James Cone contend that these songs were religious hymns that also signaled rebellion, social critique, and concepts of freedom for enslaved Blacks in the face of inhumane treatment.[50] The spirituals represent a genuine folk music because the songs became enshrined as a most unique oral tradition within American culture. The words varied from region to region because song leaders found it necessary to improvise lyrics they either had forgotten or needed to change.[51]

Although enslaved African Americans were very moved by the teachings of the New Testament, the songs and spirituality they created were largely defined by the Old Testament's stories of the weak overcoming the powerful. Translating the biblical story of the liberation of Moses and the Israelites from Egyptian slavery known as "the exodus" into musical form was vitally important to encouraging enslaved African Americans that they, not the slaveholders, were unequivocally God's "Chosen People" who deserved freedom, justice, and equality.

THE BLACK CHURCH AS THE "VISIBLE INSTITUTION" IN THE ANTEBELLUM NORTH

While the invisible institution was the central aspect of Black Christian life in the South, the materialization of independent Black churches as the "visible institution" was becoming increasingly more significant in the antebellum North. Reflecting upon the nature of race relations in American churches, Gayraud Wilmore asserts:

From 1750 to 1861, there were more black and white Christians worshiping in the same congregations, proportionate to their numbers as baptized Christians, than there are today. This should not, however, be taken to imply that prior to the Civil War American churches were racially integrated. Blacks enjoyed no real freedom or equality of ecclesiastical status in either the North or the South. It never occurred to white Christians that the equality that was denied to their brothers and sisters in civil society should at least be made available to them within the church. . . . There was interracial worship before the Civil War, but it was never intended to suggest equality.[52]

In the 1800s, a majority of free Blacks had specific reasons for identifying themselves with the Methodist tradition. Most Black Methodist congregations were typically northern and urban. Significant AME congregations were those located in Baltimore; New York City; Attleboro, Pennsylvania; Salem, New Jersey; and Wilmington, Delaware. By the 1840s, the AME Church had almost three hundred congregations in the United States and Canada, with over seventeen thousand members. Frederick Douglass called them "Negro pews, on a higher and larger scale."[53] Such churches, Douglass and others maintained, were part and parcel of a segregationist spirit that divided America by skin color. Foreshadowing criticisms that would persist throughout the nineteenth and twentieth centuries, Douglass also denounced what he considered the illiteracy and anti-intellectualism of most Black ministers.

Furthermore, growing numbers of African Americans during the 1800s (even Douglass would eventually affiliate himself with the AME Zion Church) regarded such churches as crucial sources of cultural pride, spiritual renewal, and social dignity while also serving as a legitimate alternative to the racial prejudice and mistreatment of their white Christian counterparts. The Methodist denominations had great appeal to a growing number of Northern Blacks because their practices of personal sanctification and what historian Evelyn Brooks Higginbotham refers to as a politics of respectability were reflected in their worship style, highly ordered liturgy, closely supervised ministry, and generally prosperous memberships.[54] Simply put, the "method of the Methodists" brought a viable institutional order to Black worship without losing the authenticity of Black spirit-filled worship.

During the first half of the nineteenth century, the Second Great Awakening significantly transformed American society and culture, and African Americans were central to this dynamic change. Regardless of race, American evangelicals were motivated to carry Christian morality into politics by inspiring a new era of revivalism in America by emphasizing a sense of "practical Christianity." In keeping with their beliefs, they felt that those who were truly saved would not be content with their own salvation. Rather, they would want to help save others. In particular, Black evangelicals of this period called for "a *liberating* faith" that would advance both material and spiritual well-being.

Ever since the nation's founding, African American religious leaders and institutions were engaged in multiple roles and purposes as well as rich discursive practices that represented an effort during the antebellum era to create an independent and robust Black political sphere. In the struggle to resist slavery and white supremacy, Black Northerners in a state of quasi freedom developed a radically exclusive notion of Blackness as a collective racial identity as well as a revolutionary sense of nationhood as both a secular and sacred priority. By way of illustration, Richard Allen and Absalom Jones founded the Free African Society, which served not only as a religious group but also as a mutual aid society and fraternal organization with a whole host of other features to satisfy the pressing social needs of the local Black community in Philadelphia. Additionally, David Walker, the fiercely outspoken Black abolitionist and author of the famous *Appeal to the Coloured Citizens of the World* (1829), was both a Boston distributor for the *Freedom's Journal* as well as a lay minister serving in the AME Church.

During the early 1800s, free Blacks viewed the emergence of the Black press as a major step forward and their collective concerns outside the confines of an antagonistic mainstream media as a way to define their community for themselves. Samuel Cornish and John B. Russwurm founded the nation's first Black-controlled newspaper, *Freedom's Journal*, on March 12, 1827. They stated in their masthead that the paper was "devoted to the improvement of the colored population." They noted that blacks had been "incorrectly represented by the press and the church. Their faults were always noted but their virtues remain unmentioned."[55] From 1820 to 1860, there were nearly half a million free "colored people" in the United States, and the publishers anticipated that at least half of them would read the journal. The paper's publication lasted until 1830, but its influence resonated and transcended beyond the era.

In the 1830s, Black Methodists, under the leadership of AME Bishop Allen, initiated the National Negro Convention Movement, a series of official semiannual gatherings. These gatherings were places where Black representatives met across the boundaries of religious denomination, class, educational status, region, and eventually gender in order to strategize ways to maximize prospects for Black independence, whether in the United States or elsewhere. Moreover, the participants in the National Negro Convention Movement were intently focused on the importance of creating and maintaining autonomous institutions because they allowed Blacks to cultivate a sense of unity within the nascent free Black community of the North. Through cooperative, if not always coordinated, efforts, African American institutions such as African schools, independent Black churches, fraternal lodges, mutual aid societies, and the Black press worked together under one organizational umbrella. The National Negro Convention Movement served as a crossroads for Black civil society in what Eddie Glaude has referred to as the "secular adjunct of the black church."[56] Glaude is incredibly helpful in viewing the centrality of Black faith in nurturing what he calls "exodus politics." He sees it as being indispensable to the Black freedom struggle framed by belief in God's solidarity with the oppressed and downtrodden.

However, by the 1830s and 1840s, some Black leaders began to criticize the existence of separate Black churches, fearing their presence would create more permanent division between Black churchgoers and their white neighbors. Nevertheless, the collective identity of the free Black community in the early 1800s revolved around the independent Black Church movement, free African schools, the development of Black-owned businesses, and various burial and benevolent societies for self-help and protection against poverty, illness, and other disasters in nineteenth-century American society. In their community-building activities in the antebellum North, free Blacks wanted to create a term or identity for themselves that would allow them to retain their "African" heritage but also claim their rights as "Americans." Generally, they settled on the phrases *colored Americans* or *people of color*.

THE BLACK CHURCH AND THE ANTISLAVERY STRUGGLE

The most powerful and politically important development of the Second Great Awakening was connected to confronting the enslavement of African Americans in the United States. Abolitionists were typically people who committed themselves to ending slavery on state and national levels. The abolitionist movement actually had two expressions that continued to exist until the climax of the American Civil War. The first of these abolitionist movements existed in the antebellum South among the enslaved, with the help of the small number of free Blacks and sympathetic white people. Enslaved African Americans individually and in groups sought their liberation through violent and nonviolent means.

The second abolitionist movement was composed of white and Black antislavery advocates in the North with strategic outposts in the upper South. Although far more white people in the North were involved in the abolitionist struggle than in the South, the presence and involvement of African Americans were central to the movement's existence in serious ways. For instance, even as liberal white reformers such as William Lloyd Garrison, the Grimké sisters (Sarah and Angelina), and Theodore Weld began to dominate the larger, more renowned abolitionist organizations, free Blacks such as David Walker, Maria Stewart, Henry Highland Garnet, and others became involved in direct arguments and political action against slavery in the South in addition to slavery's influences in the North. In the upper South, however, African Americans (whether free or enslaved) could not participate in antislavery organizations, but many still cooperated covertly and informally with white abolitionists. Whether the series of failed slave revolts or the Underground Railroad, these forms of resistance to American slavery in the antebellum South made it possible for a modest number of enslaved people to free themselves yet proved unable to bring the entire institution of slavery to an end.[57]

Arguably the most radical of all antislavery documents, Walker's *Appeal* caused a great stir when it was published in September of 1829 with its call for slaves to revolt against their masters. As a free Black originally from the South, David Walker wrote, "They want us for their

54

slaves, and think nothing of murdering us . . . therefore, if there is an *attempt* made by us, kill or be killed . . . and believe this, that it is no more harm for you to kill a man who is trying to kill you, than it is for you to take a drink of water when thirsty."[58] The goal of the *Appeal* was to instill pride and courage among the Black population and give them hope that change would someday come. It also spoke out against colonization, a popular movement that sought to move free blacks to a colony in Africa. America, Walker believed, belonged to all who helped build it. He went even further, stating, "America is more our country than it is the whites—we have enriched it with our *blood and tears*." He then asked, "Will they drive us from our property and homes, which we have earned with our *blood*?"

Following on the heels of Walker's bold antislavery proclamations by a couple of years, Nat Turner's rebellion in 1831 became the most infamous revolt in the United States. As an enslaved itinerant preacher, Turner believed he was ordained by God to bring terror and devastation to the Virginia countryside in protest of slavery. Whereas Turner admitted his master was kind and trusted him, nevertheless, he killed the entire family out of sheer principle. Before the revolt ended, fifty-five whites were dead and many Blacks were killed in reprisal. Turner was caught and eventually executed after dictating a confession. Although there had been numerous slave revolts that had erupted throughout the American South ever since the colonial era, it was Turner's rebellion that struck fear in Southern whites because it indicated that the enslaved Blacks were just as diverse, unpredictable, and desperate for freedom as other humans, despite the seeming invincibility of the institution of slavery.

The Underground Railroad, which existed as a vast network of people who helped fugitive slaves escape to the North and to Canada, was not run by any single organization or person. It consisted of many individuals—whites as well as Blacks—who knew only of the local efforts to aid fugitives and not the overall operation. It effectively moved hundreds of enslaved Blacks northward each year; according to one estimate, the South lost one hundred thousand enslaved Blacks between 1810 and 1850. The number of African Americans who escaped via the Underground Railroad was relatively small compared to the overall enslaved population, largely due to nightly patrols by white vigilantes as well as legal authorities.

In 1849, Harriet Tubman escaped from her master on Maryland's eastern shore and ran to secure her own freedom. By 1860, Tubman was hailed as the "Black Moses" for leading nearly twenty trips on the Underground Railroad to aid runaway slaves out of the South, including one especially challenging journey in which she rescued her seventy-year-old parents; as the most famous "conductor" on the "railroad," she led some three hundred slaves to freedom. On one occasion, it is reported that she overheard some men reading her wanted poster, which stated that she was illiterate. She promptly pulled out a book and feigned reading it. The ploy was enough to fool the men. During the Civil War, Tubman later joined the Union Army as a scout and spy.

But beyond the legendary work of Harriet Tubman and the Underground Railroad, there was a much larger yet underemphasized phenomenon of enslaved Blacks seeking escape from bondage on their own terms. Often Blacks who escaped from various forms of slavery hid in nearby woods or swamps and went to the quarters at night for food. Often they were ultimately returned to the plantation by slave patrols. Others formed colonies of runaways in the swamps and mountains, especially in Florida, where the Seminole Indians often befriended and protected them from capture.

The independent Black churches of the antebellum North were especially significant in the abolitionist movement. With a few noteworthy exceptions, the leading Black abolitionists were ministers. Among them were Henry Highland Garnet, Theodore S. Wright, Samuel E. Cornish, Jehiel C. Berman, Charles B. Ray, James C. W. Pennington, Nathaniel Paul, Alexander Crummell, Samuel Ringgold Ward, and Daniel A. Payne. Some of these African American men were leaders of the African Baptist Church or the AME Church while others preached to Black congregations affiliated with predominantly white churches. A few Black ministers, such as Amos N. Freeman of Brooklyn, New York, served white abolitionist congregations. These clergy used their pulpits to attack slavery, racial discrimination, proslavery white churches, and the American Colonization Society (ACS).[59]

GLIMPSES OF BLACK FREEDOM IN THE MIDST OF SLAVERY

From the early 1800s, there was increased pressure from Southern politicians and planters to either deport free Blacks or enslave them. Most had no wish to free enslaved women, men, and children, and they sought to reduce the numbers of free Blacks in the country and thus help preserve the institution of slavery. The American Colonization Society (ACS) was established in 1817 as an organization that believed free Blacks should immigrate to a territory on the west coast of Africa. In 1822, the society established a settlement in West Africa that would become the independent nation of Liberia in 1847. The name *Liberia* is derived from a Latin phrase meaning "free land," with the country's capital, Monrovia, named in honor of US President James Monroe.

As one of the Black forerunners of the "Back-to-Africa" movement, Paul Cuffe saw opportunities in shipping and thought Africans and African Americans would be able to enjoy profits if they worked together to establish a shipping network of their own. Unable to interest anyone in financing his colonization scheme, Cuffe determined to finance it himself; at a personal expenditure of $4,000, Cuffe took nine free Black families to settle in Sierra Leone in 1815. As a result, such later African American leaders as Martin R. Delany and Henry Highland Garnet began to look more favorably on migration to and colonization of Africa by African Americans several decades later.

The Black Church tradition in the United States has been predicated upon the needs and desires of people of African descent to find faith anew in a land where their fate was dictated by inhuman bondage. What's more, it is in the devastating context of American slavery—from forced capture to the Middle Passage to "seasoning" to the auction block to lives of chains and toil—that the Black family first became endangered in American society. For example, Michel-Rolph Trouillot argues that planters in the Caribbean and elsewhere in the slaveholding Atlantic world typically kept thorough records of their plantations, yet there are clear indications that slave owners neglected to document the births of enslaved Black children. The rate of infant mortality amongst enslaved families was so high on some New World plantations that many slave owners did not think it was worth the time or effort to keep records of a baby born to an enslaved mother until the infant had survived to a certain age. Keeping this fact in mind, plantation records obviously lack important data about enslaved families. Therefore, historians seeking to reconstruct the history of Black families dating back to slavery face a difficult task due to such willful neglect on the part of planters all those centuries ago. Critically assessing the irony of traditional historians' dependence upon such sketchy documentary evidence, Trouillot contends that historians use their own contemporary standards when they choose to record certain events, while consciously deciding to silence other factors.[60]

Unquestionably, slave narratives serve as one of the principal sources for the contemporary study of slave religion. There are roughly 112 written works that are identified as part of the genre in American literature known as "slave narratives." The famous examples of slave narratives belong to Olaudah Equiano, Frederick Douglass, Harriet Jacobs, William "Box" Brown, Solomon Northup, and Sojourner Truth, among others; yet all are worthy of close scrutiny and examination. Only 10 percent of these accounts were written or narrated by Black women. But there are major concerns about the slave narratives: Who is the "real" author? When were they "really" written? Who is the "real" audience? What is the "real" purpose? How can they be verified in "real" terms?[61]

As the basis of modern African American history and literature, the slave narratives follow a similar three-stage pattern, beginning with either an idyllic childhood in a West African village or the relative innocence of childhood on a Southern plantation. Aimed at Northern white readers, the bulk of the stories describe, in vivid detail, the brutal oppressions of captivity and slavery, dwelling on the horrors of the slave ships, slave sales, the breakup of families, the daily beatings and punishments, and the harsh rigors of life on the plantation. Next, the narratives also describe a creative and heroic will to survive: cunning strategies for avoiding work, rebelling against one's owner, connecting with loved ones, developing a sense of spirituality, and learning how to read and write. Finally, the narratives conclude with the story of escape and the assumption of a new identity in freedom.

There are various key themes within slave narratives. During the actual heyday of slave narratives, they served as extremely poignant appeals to white readers to agitate for the abolition of slavery. The slave narratives were remarkably astute about revealing stark contrasts between the religion that slaveholders used to justify slavery and the simple and the spiritually based Christianity of enslaved Blacks themselves. The concentrated focus on the initial process of planning an escape, rather than the strict details of individual or collective oppression under slavery, was a mainstay of the slave narrative. Moreover, the overwhelming majority of slave narratives indicate the considerable restraints and anticipated difficulties of running away. The slave narratives reveal the inherent cleverness as well as organic intelligence of fugitives. Lastly, the narratives galvanized the supportive strength of the enslaved community as well as the white and black members of the Underground Railroad in successfully guiding runaways to freedom.

Alternately, the Ex-Slave Narratives were compiled in the 1930s by the efforts of social researchers funded by the Federal Works Project. While this collection of oral-history interviews was initiated roughly a decade earlier by special research programs by historically Black colleges and universities such as Hampton Institute and Fisk University, the cadre of social researchers sponsored by the New Deal government amassed a collection of several thousand interviews of Black women and men who were formerly enslaved. For the purpose of expanding our understanding of slave religiosity, these classic and modern sources are extremely invaluable in acquiring greater insights into the sacred worldview and quest for spiritual liberation and social freedom.[62] As primary documentary evidence, most slave narratives are notable for how they demonstrate the thoughts and feelings of the enslaved, as they articulated their moral outrage through their religious experiences, which they recorded in these testimonials.

Recounting his time in slavery, one freed Black man was taken aback when asked about whether his former slave master had been kind. "Kind!" the emancipated man responded bitterly to this remark and continued:

I was dat man's slave; and he sold my wife, and he sold my two chill'en. . . . Kind! yes, he gib me corn enough, and he gib me pork enough, and he neber gib me one lick wid de whip but whar's my wife?—whar's my chill'en? Take away de pork, I say; take away de corn, I can work and raise dese for myself; but gib me back de wife of my bosom, and gib me back my poor chill'en as was sold away.[63]

In that narrative, the man's story sets a completely different standard for the concept of "life, liberty, and the pursuit of happiness" that has nothing to do with fame, revenge, or wealth. After all was said and done, he merely wanted the restoration of his family, despite the reality of being a victim of the American social order that found his family unworthy of governmental protection or God's love.

Needless to say, nothing provided greater substance for the abolitionists' attacks against chattel slavery than the existence of Black families. Throughout the Old South, the legal system neither recognized nor protected the sanctity of Black marriages or legitimate slave family ties. Meanwhile, slave owners were free to sell enslaved spouses away from one another, separate parents from children, sexually exploit Black women and daughters, and generally disrupt the structure of slave families in whatever ways benefited the needs of the master. To be sure, countless slave owners believed that it was in their own self-interest to encourage some modicum of stable Black families as a source of renewable wealth and a sense of personal security. Plantation owners and slave masters commented that they felt that providing a semblance of stability among enslaved Black families functioned to raise morale as well as reduce the likelihood of enslaved Blacks running away or inciting revolts. Nevertheless, contemporary readers must always understand that slave owners showed concern about Black marriage and family in the antebellum South because they considered the enslaved as being a form of property, and rarely was their concern out of any genuine sense of humane treatment or Christian charity. For instance, when conducting marriages between the enslaved, slave owners deliberately avoided any wording that indicated the state of Black matrimony was a perpetual union. This occurred for two reasons: first, slave owners held the right to sell either spouse at their discretion; second, this distinction cast Black marriages as unquestionably inferior to those of white married couples. By way of illustration, numerous ex-slave narratives recounted that masters never said, "What God has joined together, let no one put asunder" during the officiating of slave marriages, but instead simply said, "Now you married."[64] As one enslaved preacher states, slave owners should have concluded slave marriage ceremonies with the phrase: "Till death or buckra [master] do you part."[65]

Despite the possibility of disruption, enslaved Black folk were passionately committed to their families. One sign of the ties that bind is revealed in the tendency of enslaved parents to name their children after ancestors or relatives in order to perpetuate a sense of familial identity and unity against insurmountable odds. The enduring strength of family ties among the enslaved is also suggested by the numerous ads by slave catchers that indicated that enslaved fugitives had escaped in all likelihood in order to visit family members on far-flung plantations. Thankfully through the documentary evidence provided by slave narratives and letters, we have a graphic record of enslaved families' commitment to one another. One enslaved man, Abream Scriven, after learning that he was going to be sold away from his family, wrote to his wife: "My dear wife for you and my Children my pen cannot Express the [grief] I feel to [be] parted from you all. . . . I remain truly your husband until Death."[66] In another instance, George Pleasant, an enslaved man located in Tennessee, expressed his deepest thoughts and greatest wishes regarding his wife who was enslaved in North Carolina: "I hope with God's helpe that I may be abble to rejoys with you on the earth and In heaven lets meet when [God] will [sic]."[67] These and other examples reflect that there was deep care and concern for Black people who, although enslaved, could find ways to love wife, husband, mother, father, son, daughter, sister, brother, and every other manifestation of kin (both factual and fictive) in meaningful and intentional ways in spite of the yoke of bondage.

Taking this issue even higher, the ability for any notion of Black love to survive chattel slavery was a radical act. Toward this end, I think back to a classic passage of Toni Morrison's novel *Beloved* in which Sethe, the book's protagonist, yearns to go to the clearing where her mother-in-law, Baby Suggs, used to preach. In Morrison's imagined rendition of the hush harbor, Baby Suggs did not necessarily give sermons so much as provide pastoral care and practical wisdom by instructing the crowds of enslaved Black folks to laugh, dance, and love their bodies, in particular their hearts and mouths. Free from the immediate surveillance of slave masters or the lash of an overseer's whip, she told her makeshift congregation: "Here . . . in this here place, we flesh; flesh that weeps, laughs; flesh that dances on bare feet in grass. Love it. Love it hard."[68]

Building on what some might refer to as the "audacity of hope," Morrison channels the urgent thoughts that kept so many millions of enslaved women, men, and children strong in mind, body, and spirit, despite dreadful conditions and hateful actions that were intended to tear them down. Long before the fateful collapse of the institution of slavery, enslaved Black folk made their way toward freedom by declaring themselves as being truly beloved both individually and collectively.

What is important to remember is that the first half of the nineteenth century witnessed the massive expansion and consolidation of chattel slavery in the United States, and, along with family and socialization, religion helped enslaved Black men, women, and children survive the "peculiar institution."[69] Some slave masters denied enslaved Blacks access to Protestant Christianity because they feared the prospect that African Americans would seek manumission and racial equality as a result of prolonged exposure to the gospel. Meanwhile, some of the enslaved Black populace actively ignored Christianity because they could not embrace the professed religion of white Americans.

In addition to performing religious functions and guarding moral discipline and community values, the era's Black churches provided and promoted education, social insurance, fraternal associations, and recreation. Besides revolving around the church, the collective identity of the free Black community also revolved around the African schools and various burial and benevolent societies for self-help and protection against poverty, illness, and other disasters. By the 1850s, the growing concern of Southerners with the presence of free Blacks in their midst led to the threat of extinction for the free Black community. Pressures increased to either deport free Blacks or enslave them. As a result, some Black leaders, such as prototypical Black nationalists Martin R. Delany and Henry Highland Garnet, began to look more favorably on migration to and colonization of Africa by African Americans. But that quest was interrupted by the outbreak of the Civil War.[70]

RACE, RELIGION, AND THE AMERICAN CIVIL WAR

For Blacks and whites alike, religion played a significant role in the broad sweep of events that led to the Civil War. Religion was also important during the war itself and was even important in the struggle for definition and meaning in the war's aftermath. White mainline Christians in both the North and the South looked to their churches, their faith, and their religious leaders as a means of justifying their viewpoints on the matter of slavery, and, as the war broke out, they sought God's will and redemptive power to sustain them in the midst of the terrible violence and horrific bloodshed that pitted one American against another. Once battle lines were drawn, neighbors, friends, and kin fought against one another. White Americans on either side of the Mason-Dixon Line felt that God was certainly on their side and that they were fighting on behalf of righteousness; subsequently, they knew without a doubt that God was going to give them victory. This largely meant that both sides of the conflict sought to demonstrate how Christian scriptures vindicated their cause over and against their opposition. The historical accounts of the Civil War offer a stirring record of the unmitigated inhumanity of war unleashed upon the American populace.[71]

What most often gets obscured in conversations about the American Civil War is that religious perspectives were critically important to the foment of the conflict. For example, the proslavery advocates had amassed a wide array of justifications for the preservation of chattel slavery as an essential component of the Southern cultural and economic composition. One of the principal claims was the historical justification, which argued that slavery had existed throughout history and that the greatest civilizations had built their strength and grandeur on slave labor. Next, there was also a legalistic justification advanced during this period that stated that the US Constitution did not forbid slavery but

63

implied its constitutionality in the "Three-fifths Clause," the section protecting the overseas slave trade for twenty years and mandating the return of runaways. As early as the 1830s, a pseudoscientific justification contended that white Southerners had been created separately and that Africans were an inherently inferior race, destined to serve the superior Caucasians. Next, in a similar vein, there was an emerging sociological justification that espoused the view that Blacks needed the paternal guidance, restraint, and protection of white masters. If those were lacking, chaos would result. Most important, however, is the biblical and theological justification wherein white proslavery Christians argued that the "Curse of Ham" (Gen. 9:18-27) in the Hebrew Bible as well as the New Testament pronouncements on slavery (Luke 12:47; Eph. 6:5-8) provided the divine rationale for the unyielding enslavement of Black women, men, and children.

Alternately, the abolitionist cause also had notable responses to the horrific institution of slavery and the Civil War that were rooted in mainline American religious thought. By way of illustration, it was Harriet Beecher Stowe's classic antislavery novel, *Uncle Tom's Cabin*, that was deeply influenced by her Congregationalist faith. Furthermore, in the context of a war that literally split the nation in half, James Russell Lowell's song "Once to Every Man and Nation," familiar to a majority of mainline Protestants, served as a reminder of the pronouncements of the ancient Hebrew prophets that people must make a definitive decision in the choice between good and evil. Finally and most powerfully, Julia Ward Howe's "Battle Hymn of the Republic" spoke in such stirring and eloquent terms of God's unwavering judgment on people who made wrong choices in the service of evil, wickedness, and oppression that it eventually became an anthem of the Union cause.

What must be understood is that African Americans—whether free or enslaved—did not side with the Union because of abstract notions of federal authority versus states' rights or industrial capitalism versus agricultural economy. The significance of the Civil War within the African American experience was defined by the insurmountable struggle to liberate all people of African descent and make certain that freedom, justice, and equality would be the rightful property of them and their progeny.[72] As the foremost advocate for the all-Black Fifty-

Fourth Massachusetts Colored Infantry, Frederick Douglass once encouraged the growing throngs of Black folk to "remember that in a contest with oppression, the Almighty has no attribute which can take sides with oppressors."[73]

Another interesting development that became a prevalent aspect of the Civil War's lasting impact on the Black Church tradition was the Watch Night service on New Year's Eve. According to Methodist practice, a Watch Night was a church meeting that had singing, prayer, and preaching that began late in the evening and continued until shortly after midnight on New Year's Day. What was otherwise a generic worship activity now took on ultimate significance for every member of the African American community in the United States on December 31, 1862. In heavy anticipation of President Lincoln's signing the decree (later known as the Emancipation Proclamation) conferring freedom to all African Americans, the Watch Night services were coordinated in order to be held particularly for Black women, men, and children in all churches in the North as well as in the South. Since the first so-called Emancipation Day, Watch Night services on New Year's Eve became a staple within countless Black churches, regardless of denominational affiliation, as a commemoration of the event that marked the beginning of slavery's end.

By the time President Abraham Lincoln signed the Emancipation Proclamation on January 1, 1863, Union forces were facing incredible numbers of casualities and had a desperate need for more troops. This need may have inspired the North's political and military leadership to put African Americans in the blue soldiers' garb of the Union Army. When this opportunity arose, hundreds of thousands of Black men and women in the North and even in the South leapt at the chance to strike a fatal blow against chattel slavery.

THE END OF THE CIVIL WAR AND THE BIRTH OF BLACK FREEDOM

Although the Civil War was not the first American conflict in which Black soldiers fought, it was the first war that allowed African

Americans to serve as chaplains. In this tumultuous struggle to end slavery in the United States, the African American chaplain had a very demanding task concerning the physical and spiritual maintenance of the Black troops gathering to the Union cause. Each chaplain was assigned to a regiment of one thousand soldiers. Therefore, 180 chaplains attended to the religious needs of nearly 180,000 Black troops enlisted by the Union forces from 1863 to 1865; of the 180 chaplains meeting the spiritual needs of Black regiments, only fourteen were African Americans. These chaplains did much more that lead worship for the troops.[74] In addition to their pastoral duties—such as visiting the sick and wounded, holding prayer meetings, and burying the dead—the chaplain often had to ensure that wounded Black troops received medical care and had to guarantee that soldiers' pay was sent to their next of kin. Moreover, since Black chaplains were usually the only Black commissioned officers in their regiments, they often became advocates and intermediaries for Black troops in many dealings with their commanding officers.

In his examination of the centrality of religion in the communities of enslaved Blacks in the South during the Civil War era, Eugene Genovese reveals how all-encompassing the religious experience of African Americans is, especially in the face of battle:

> White contemporaries . . . agreed that the religious life of the slaves embraced much more than religion, anything they were capable of recognizing as Christianity. Most also agreed that the slaves' religious feeling, whatever its elements, ran deep. During the war Thomas Wentworth Higginson recounted with wonder and admiration the spirit of the black troops, most of whom had only recently been slaves. Not since Cromwell's time, he exulted, have we seen so religious an army. The blacks called it a "Gospel Army." Among the more significant features of his account are these: the blacks spoke and sang incessantly of Moses and associated him with all the great events of history, including the most recent; their services displayed drumming, clapping, and bodily movement in the African manner; and the praisehouses they built reminded him of nothing so much as a "regular African hut." He observed wisely that the deep religious faith of the slaves had saved them from the dehumanization the abolitionists had feared inevitable under slavery.[75]

66

Equally remarkable is the fact that prior to the Civil War, most white Americans generally did not know anything about the spirituals. This discovery was largely an outgrowth of Black soldiers gathering around nightly campfires and singing their spirituals for solace and strength under the watchful eye of their white counterparts.[76] What is most astonishing about this observation by white onlookers was that, in an armed conflict that had so much to do with race and religion, white Americans lacked any genuine knowledge of Black faith and spirituality.

When word of their emancipation was spread amongst the enslaved Black populace of the American South following January 1, 1863, historian W. E. B. DuBois indicates that the majority of them "were in religious and hysterical fervor. This was the coming of the Lord. This was the fulfillment of prophecy and legend. It was the Golden Dawn. . . . It was everything miraculous and perfect and promising."[77] This was the substance of the Black experience of liberation in the aftermath of the Emancipation Proclamation and later when the Thirteenth Amendment was ratified on January 31, 1865—legislation that abolished slavery in the United States finally and forever. Amid the dizzying and devastating events of the Civil War, DuBois further states:

> To these black folk it was the Apocalypse. The magnificent trumpet tones of Hebrew Scripture, transmuted and oddly changed, became a strange new gospel. All that was Beauty, all that was Love, all that was Truth, stood on the top of these mad mornings, and sang with the stars. A great human sob shrieked in the wind, and tossed its tears upon the sea—free, free, free.[78]

Even as the Civil War aroused great hopes for freedom amongst the enslaved, it is unquestionable that the outbreak of the conflict profoundly transformed most Americans' understanding of human mortality, grief, and mourning. It must not be forgotten that the sheer carnage resulting from the war—more than six hundred thousand deaths due to combat—made the Civil War a traumatic turning point in the collective national consciousness.[79] Despite all the attempts to create lines of division and hierarchy, the mounting death tolls over the course of the conflict helped illuminate once and for all that death is the great inescapable equalizer of all humankind. The staggering number of causalities caused a crisis of faith that demanded new, better ways for dealing with the overwhelming specter of death as well as the crushing weight of grief that inevitably followed such a wholesale loss of human life.

For all Americans, regardless of race or region, the massive body count forced them to wrestle with their most deeply held convictions and beliefs about how to properly honor the fallen soldiers while also dealing with the grisly and often drawn-out death on the battlefield. Moreover, as the war drew to its eventual, albeit bloody, conclusion, formerly enslaved Black women, men, and children began to lay claim to their newly gained freedom; and the hush harbors that sustained them during slavery soon became unnecessary vestiges of an undesirable past. Although many features of those sacred gatherings would not disappear altogether following the end of the war, the declining significance of such communal acts did begin to fade as the newly emancipated blacks began to develop their own independent religious and spiritual lives.

As the battlefields cleared and the soldiers' guns fell silent in April 1865, both the Union and Confederacy quickly sought to invoke the religious notions of divine punishment and wrath, on the one hand, and the spiritual overtones of righteousness and sacrifice, on the other, in order to construe the meaning of the Civil War and to understand the victory won or defeat suffered. Faced with the ambiguous nature of their newly gained freedom, Black women, men, and children were able to face the future with the courage tested by war and with a hope buoyed by the arrival of that miraculous manifestation of answered prayers—emancipation.

chapter 2

MAKING AMERICA AGAIN

The Black Church Tradition from Segregation to the Civil Rights Movement

Let America be the dream the dreamers dreamed . . .

Langston Hughes, "Let America Be America Again"

In the poem "Let America Be America Again," Langston Hughes describes a vision of the American dream that never has existed for the majority of Americans. It is about the freedom, dignity, and equality that every person in this society looks forward to but fears may never be realized in his or her lifetime. Even as forces of brutal oppression and unconscionable exclusion would come to bear upon much of mainstream America during his lifetime, in this poem Hughes represents the demands and desires not only of African Americans but also of other marginalized and oppressed peoples, all of whom seek some measure of America's great promise to call their own. Even as Hughes lambasts the pervasive nature of injustice in American life, the poem also articulates the belief that the American Dream can be achieved someday.

By the mid-1860s, the development of Black religion blossomed exponentially with the dawn of freedom. The emphasis of this era focused most intently upon the establishment of justice for each member of American society. The fervor of emancipation for America's newly freed citizenry had to be tempered, however, with grim realities

69

of continued social oppression and repressive legislation that Blacks would face from the end of the Civil War to the aftermath of the civil rights movement. Although the Emancipation Proclamation and the ratification of the Thirteenth Amendment of the US Constitution abolished slavery throughout the former Confederacy, such laws could not dismantle the racial antipathy that would gradually coalesce into the system of racial segregation that would condemn Black women, men, and children to second-class citizenship during the long century of struggle.

As President Abraham Lincoln implored his fellow Americans to become a nation and people "with malice toward none, with charity for all, with firmness in the right as God gives us to see the right," during his second inaugural address and as the Thirteenth Amendment awaited ratification, more than fifty thousand enslaved Black wives and children had already been set free. In a world undergoing profound change forged during the crucible of war, the constitutional abolition of slavery fused with the ostensible freedom endowed by marriage and the enduring domestic bonds of family, thereby bringing forth "a new birth of freedom" that wedded civil rights to human rights. Although we do not often discuss them in this fashion, the Thirteenth Amendment and the ensuing civil rights legislation were acts of liberation that split asunder the legally protected relationship between master and slave, effectively legally destroying the concept of human beings as chattel property. By changing chattel into free people by means of constitutional amendment amid the devastating crisis of the Civil War, the United States suddenly belonged to a tradition amongst former slave societies of declaring rights that invalidated unjust forms of sovereignty that had emerged throughout the Atlantic world during the "Age of Revolution."[1] This was most evident when tens of thousands of formerly enslaved Blacks sought to express their new rights as citizens by getting married—a sociopolitical phenomenon that extended from Haiti to Jamaica to the American South to Brazil at the onset of freedom.[2]

In the wake of emancipation, the various historically Black Baptist and Methodist denominations headed southbound in order to execute the most robust and thriving campaign amongst the newly emancipated Black populace of the American South. Exclusion of freed Blacks from mainline Protestant denominations meant that these Black faith communities witnessed a sizable increase in membership thanks to their intentional initiative. However, mainline denominations remained mostly segregated, contributing greatly to the establishment of all-Black congregations and worship styles even within predominantly white denominations. Even Roman Catholicism grew due to an increase of Black Catholics in locales such as Louisiana and Maryland. As a result, the definitive core of the historic Black Church tradition was firmly set in place with its own distinctive cultural styles and theological imperatives.

In the North as well as in the South, the rising tide of Black churches played a particular role in the transformation of Black communities both in rural areas and in major cities. More than simply being religious institutions, churches also helped African Americans adapt to the new options that welcomed them as they sought better prospects for their lives in terms of work and well-being. In their study of the Black Church tradition in the United States, sociologists C. Eric Lincoln and Lawrence Mamiya describe this situation as follows:

> The black church has no challenger as the cultural womb of the black community. Not only did it give birth to new institutions such as schools, banks, insurance companies, and low income housing, it also provided an academy and an arena for political activities, and it nurtured young talent for musical, dramatic, and artistic development . . . in addition to the traditional concerns of worship, moral nurture, education, and social control. Much of black culture is heavily indebted to the black religious tradition, including most forms of black music, drama, literature, storytelling, and even humor.[3]

As Lincoln and Mamiya suggest, although Black churches have proven themselves to be much more than occasional houses of worship, the functionality of these institutions in the lives of African Americans since Reconstruction is still undeniably rooted in their primary identification as religious entities. Black churches during this pivotal era, as historian Sydney Ahlstrom notes, also served as a "surrogate for nationality" wherein religious affiliation stood as a substitute for a lost sense of collective identity as a direct result of enslavement.[4]

71

THE EVOLUTION OF THE MODERN BLACK CHURCH TRADITION AFTER EMANCIPATION

The evolution of the historic Black Church tradition in America since emancipation can be discussed in two ways. Most generally and popularly, the Black Church is any Christian congregation predominantly populated by Blacks, including all European-founded and European-governed Christian congregations (that is, Southern Baptist, American Baptist, Presbyterian, Episcopalian, Lutheran, Roman Catholic, Seventh-Day Adventists, Assemblies of God, Pentecostal, Methodist, and so on). However, most scholarly literature defined the Black Church as the conglomeration of specific Protestant denominations that was created, founded, governed, and populated overwhelmingly by Blacks. This model reflects an organized religiosity that merges doctrines of faith with an unapologetic cultural and political awareness in order to be intentionally relevant to the social plight and spiritual desires of African Americans. Taken together, the first seven denominations—the African Methodist Episcopal (A.M.E.) Church; the African Methodist Episcopal Zion (A.M.E.Z.) Church; the Christian Methodist Episcopal (C.M.E.) Church; the National Baptist Convention, U.S.A., Incorporated (NBC); the National Baptist Convention, U.S.A., Unincorporated (NBCA); the Progressive National Baptist Convention (PNBC); and the Church of God in Christ (COGIC)—accounted for more than eighty percent of all Black Christians during the first half of the twentieth century. Just as the Black Church tradition in the antebellum South was hailed as the "invisible institution" that helped millions of African Americans survive slavery in this country, the modern Black church in the North in the late nineteenth and early twentieth centuries ought to be considered the "visible institution." Northern Black churches during this period helped hundreds of thousands of Black migrants adjust to urban life while affirming an enduring set of core values consisting of freedom, justice, and equality with an abiding pride in a common racial identity for the entire Black community.

In the years after slavery was abolished, the historic Black Church tradition became the most important institution among African Americans other than the family. Not only did churches fill deep spiritual and inspirational needs but also they offered enriching music, provided charity and compassion to the needy, developed community and political leaders, and were free of white supervision. Before slavery's demise, free and enslaved Black people often attended white churches. Although these Black Christians were encouraged to participate in church services conducted by white ministers, racist white churchgoers treated them shabbily.

Beginning as early as the eighteenth century, historian Albert Raboteau identifies in Black religion a general departure from the notion that white Christians in America were simply not living up to their nation's creedal promises. As Raboteau indicates, as the primacy and durability of racism proved increasingly intransigent, Black Christians began to recognize that the creed itself was wrong. By the end of the nineteenth century, however, many Black clergy viewed the onslaught of racial discrimination not as an anomaly "in the overall progress of national destiny" but rather as a central failure of the great American experiment. By this token, the social teachings of the Black Church tradition instilled in its membership the notion that Black Christianity entailed a messianic vision of moral leadership, a mission that ostensibly "contradicted the national myth."[5]

Once liberated from bondage, the freed people eventually organized their own churches with their own ministers. Most freed Blacks considered white ministers incapable of preaching a meaningful message befitting their reality. In the wake of her emancipation, formerly enslaved Nancy Williams commented, "Ole white preachers used to talk wid day tongues widdout saying nothin', but Jesus told us slaves to talk wid our hearts."[6] In the meantime, even though many Black preachers had been denied access to formal education, they nevertheless communicated powerfully and passionately with their parishioners in a manner that sometimes appalled Northern white missionaries. Despite such denouncements, white missionaries and other observers could not deny the visible impact of Black preachers on their congregation. For instance, a visiting white clergyman was genuinely impressed and humbled upon hearing the stellar sermons of one of these unlettered Black preachers whose devout faith more than compensated for any lack of formal education. This onlooker later recalled: "He talked about Christ and his salvation as one who understood what he said. . . . Here was an unlearned man, one who could not read, telling of the love of Christ, of Christian faith and duty in a way which I have not learned."[7]

Other Black and white religious leaders anguished over what they considered moral laxity and displaced values among the freed people. The ministers preached about temperance, thrift, honesty, integrity, and the eradication of sexual promiscuity, moral attitudes that were very much in keeping with the ethos of Victorian-era America. They demanded an end to "rum-suckers, bar-room loafers, whiskey dealers and card players among the men, and to those women who dressed finely on ill gotten gain."[8]

Aside from the federal government's efforts through the Freedmen's Bureau, concerned private citizens, both Black and white, went into the American South to provide material assistance and educational opportunities to newly freed African Americans. Founded by the Congregational Church, the American Missionary Association (AMA) had a major impact in helping the freed people make a smoother transition from slavery to emancipation.[9] The Black churches became integral to the struggle to help Black women, men, and children adapt to their new future.

For Black and white Northern teachers alike migrating to the South after the Civil War, education was considered to have a deeply moral component. As essential as it was to teach Black Southerners how to read, write, and "figure" (the ability to know and do arithmetic), these same educators also believed that schools could extol moral virtues and social values such as honesty, punctuality, discipline, thrift, and temperance.[10] All of this was meant to make their students better citizens. In spite of nagging poverty, culture shock, and the escalation of violent backlash by whites, the missionary zeal of teachers as well as the enthusiasm of the freed people was able to help develop Black freedmen's schools as symbols of freedom and empowerment. Second only to the immediate need for food, clothes, and shelter, education was the most sought after need by emancipated African Americans. Nevertheless, while the belief that acquiring proficiency in reading, writing, and arithmetic granted Black folk a greater sense of their freedom, they also believed that education ensured that their greatest desire—the ability to read the Bible for themselves—could be fulfilled.

Apart from their obvious task of providing higher education and moral instruction, educational institutions that eventually became known as historically Black colleges and universities (HBCUs) were laying the foundation for the creation of an educated Black middle class. From humble roots, many of these freedmen's schools evolved gradually into the basis of the HBCUs. Many of these schools were founded and supported by white and Black churches such as Shaw University (1865), Morehouse College (1867), and Bishop College (1881) by the Baptists; Morgan State University—formerly known as Morgan College (1867)—and Bennett College (1873) by the Methodists; Fisk University (1866), Talladega College (1867), and Hampton University (1868) by the AMA; Knoxville College (1875) by the Presbyterians; Wilberforce University (1863) and Morris Brown College (1885) by the AME Church; and Livingstone College (1879) by the AME Zion Church. By the end of the nineteenth century, these institutions became the foremost sources of African American professionals, especially in terms of ministers, who were overwhelmingly Black men, and teachers, who were mostly Black women.

As a prominent Black religious leader and pioneering pan-African intellectual, Alexander Crummell advocated that America's Black populace should commit itself to missionary activities on the African continent. Ordained as an Episcopalian priest in the United States, Crummell went to England in the late 1840s to raise money for his church back home by lecturing about American slavery. In turn, abolitionists supported his three years of study at the University of Cambridge. Throughout his life, he developed concepts of pan-Africanism such as racial solidarity, self-help, and separate economic development. In 1853 he moved to Liberia, where he worked to convert native Africans to Christianity and educate them, as well as to persuade American colonists of his ideas. He lived and worked in Liberia for twenty years. During that time, he frequently appealed to Black Americans to join him but did not gather wide support for his ideas. Upon his return to the United States in the early 1870s, he and his congregation founded St. Luke's Episcopal Church, the first independent Black Episcopal church in the District of Columbia, where he served as rector until his retirement in 1894.

Organized in 1897 in Washington, DC, the Lott Carey Baptist Foreign Mission Convention (LCC) became the first independent foreign mission society founded by African Americans. Focused specifically on advancing the goals of Christian ministry, education, and health in Africa, the LCC was named in memory of Lott Carey, a freed Black preacher and pioneering missionary. In the late 1800s, Black churches lacked the resources and were ill equipped to sponsor large-scale Christianizing missions to Africa. Nonetheless, such efforts by African American Christians were important because they symbolized a spiritual redemption of their ancestral homeland. Presently, boasting the participation of three thousand churches and at least one hundred full-time workers overseas, the Lott Carey Convention (LCC) became the premier African American missionary organization focusing on issues of health care, education, poverty, and spirituality in Africa, Asia, the Caribbean, Europe, and Latin America.[11]

BLACK DENOMINATIONALISM AND THE CONSOLIDATION OF THE "BLACK CHURCH" IN MODERN AMERICA

In the post–Civil War American South, a region that had banned Black religious practice by law as well as by force, most of the newly freed men, women, and children founded Baptist and Methodist churches. These denominations tended to be more autonomous and less subject to outside control. Members of African American churches struggled, scrimped, and saved to buy land and build churches. Moreover, their embrace of Christian doctrine was usually simple and direct without a complex, articulated theology. Of the Methodist denominations, the AME Church made giant strides in the South after the Civil War. For instance, the AME church in Charleston, South Carolina, was resurrected after an absence of more than forty years.

In 1822, during the tumult over the foiled Denmark Vesey slave revolt, the lone AME church in Charleston was forced to disband and its leader had to flee. But, by the 1870s, there were three thriving AME congregations in Charleston. In another example, there were some 1,600 members of the Front Street Methodist Church in Wilmington, North Carolina, who decided to join the AME Church soon after the Civil War ended. To further emphasize their desire to fully link their racial and religious identity as a church, the members found a Black minister to replace the longtime white pastor.

Faced with the growing attraction of the AME and AME Zion denominations in the post–Civil War South, white members of the Methodist Episcopal Church South (MECS) initially encouraged cooperation with Black Methodists and helped establish the Colored Methodist Episcopal (CME) Church in 1870. Not only did the MECS eagerly ordain William H. Miles and Richard V. Vanderhost, the first CME bishops during that selfsame year, but also the MECS surrendered all property claims to the churches where CME congregations gathered and worshiped. But the white Methodists lost some of their fervor for this endeavor after they tried but failed to persuade the Black Methodists to keep political issues out of the CME church, preferring that they dwell solely on spiritual matters. In 1954, the CME Church shed the title "Colored" and renamed itself the Christian Methodist Episcopal Church. Although the CME Church certainly has been able to expand its territorial reach beyond its roots in the segregationist South by having churches in every corner of the nation, the CME continues to have the smallest membership of the three major African American Methodist denominations.

The Presbyterian, Congregational, and Episcopal churches generally appealed to the more prosperous members of the African American community. Their services tended to be more formal and solemn. Black people who had been free before the Civil War were usually affiliated with these congregations and remained so long after the conflict ended. Well-to-do freed people organized St. Mark's Protestant Episcopal Church in Charleston, South Carolina, when they separated from the white Episcopal Church, but they retained Joseph Seabrook, a white minister, as their rector. Poorer Black people generally found churches like St. Mark's unwelcoming because of a growing division over what should be considered Black Christianity in its most genuine sense.

Black churches and their parishioners and clergy would play a vital role in Reconstruction politics. More than one hundred Black ministers were elected to political office after the Civil War. By the end of the 1800s, in a world in which white supremacy and racial segregation dominated the lives and limited the possibilities of African Americans, the historic Black Church was the most important institution, alongside the family, that African Americans possessed and controlled for themselves. Numbering well over 1.3 million congregants in 1890, the South had more Black Baptists than all other denominations combined (AME Zion had 366,000, AME had 310,000, CME and other Methodists had 125,000, and Presbyterians had 114,000).[12] This huge disparity was probably attributed to the fact that the Baptist churches were congregational in nature, thus making them more independent and less bound by formal supervision and church hierarchy than other denominations. By comparison, bishops in both the AME and AME Zion denominations exercised considerable authority over congregations, as did Methodist and Presbyterian leaders. Interestingly, many Southerners, both Black and white, preferred the greater autonomy found in Baptist churches. But whereas the vast majority of Black Southerners belonged to Baptist, Methodist, and Presbyterian congregations in the late nineteenth century, it should be noted that there were probably fifteen thousand Black Episcopalians and possibly two hundred thousand Black Roman Catholics.

Denominational affiliation notwithstanding, the church was integral to the lives of most Black people in the United States. Obviously, it can be assumed that the church satisfied the spiritual needs of the African American community through what historian W. E. B. DuBois declared to be the key strengths of the historic Black Church, namely "the Preacher, the Music, and the Frenzy."[13] But, more than that, Black churches gave African American men, women, and children the opportunity, free from white surveillance, interference, and governance, to discuss, plan, organize, and lead their own community. Though church members usually had little money to spare, they tithed and contributed heartily to benevolent causes such as helping the sick, the bereaved, and the victims of natural disasters. Black congregations helped thousands of young people attend school as well as college through fund-raising, establishing scholarships, and providing care packages for needful students. Quite aptly, historian James M. Washington noted that the Black Church tradition could be defined as a "church with the soul of a nation."[14]

Although the Black Church evolved as a mainstay of the Black community, it is important to note that numerous Black congregations were plagued by sexism with detrimental effects on Black women. Women's roles and contributions in making the Black Church the most dynamic and influential institution within the African American experience have been immeasurable.[15] Female parishioners in Black churches immersed themselves deeply into church activities and proved vital to the very existence of the Black Church tradition. There has been, however, the impending challenge posed by the prospect of empowering Black women to assume ministerial roles in churches. In the earliest days of the AME Church, when Jarena Lee felt she was called to preach, she approached Richard Allen and was given a lukewarm and somewhat disturbing response. Despite his recognition of her abilities to preach, the AME bishop argued that there was no precedent in the *Book of Discipline* for the ordination of women as preachers, thus leaving her unable to fulfill her potential for a life of ministry. As Lee once argued, "If the man may preach, because the Saviour died for him, why not the woman? Seeing he died for her also. Is he not a whole Saviour instead of half one? As those who hold it wrong for a woman to preach, would seem to make It appear."[16] Sometimes, though infrequently, Black women led congregations in the late nineteenth and early twentieth centuries. For instance, the marked success of the AME Zion Church in its membership ranks was likely related to its acceptance of women in ordained ministry, as demonstrated by the ordination of Rev. Julia Foote as a minister in 1894 and Rev. Mary Jane Small as an elder a few years later. In fact, it must be noted that the AME Zion denomination embraced women's leadership long before the much older AME denomination. In spite of the pioneering efforts of female preachers like Reverend Lee, it was not until 1948 that a woman was ordained in the AME denomination.[17]

Much like the Methodist denominations, the Baptist denominations had a similar dilemma regarding the recognition of women's religious authority and spiritual gifts. In the late nineteenth century, the Black clubwomen's movement grew out of the church-based literary and self-improvement groups to enhance the lives of upper- and middle-class African American women. In its heyday from the 1890s to the 1920s, the Black clubwomen's movement transitioned from social networking and cultural pursuits to advancing the goals of social justice and political activism in the face of racial segregation. As a means of advancing the cause of greater gender inclusion (if not full-blown equality) among Black Baptists, Nannie Helen Burroughs utilized the power of the Black clubwomen's movement in order to establish Women's Day in Baptist churches in which women delivered sermons and guided the parishioners. But even Burroughs grew disgruntled and complained that Women's Day quickly became little more than an opportunity for the male pastors, deacons, and trustees to raise large sums of money instead of empowering female leadership.[18]

JIM AND JANE CROW, GREAT MIGRATION, AND THE QUEST FOR THE PROMISED LAND

For many Black Christians, the emotional involvement and enthusiastic participation in church services was an escape from their dreary and oppressive daily lives. Although he eventually became dean of Howard University School of Religion, president of Morehouse College, and mentor to an entire generation of promising Black men such as Martin Luther King Jr., Dr. Benjamin E. Mays's youth was defined by the unyielding crush of segregation resulting from the *Plessy v. Ferguson* US Supreme Court decision in 1896. Reflecting upon his childhood in Greenwood County, South Carolina, Dr. Mays recalled that Rev. James F. Marshall, a Baptist preacher in his hometown, barely had a fifth-grade education, yet the preacher "emphasized the joys of heaven and the damnation of hell" and that the "trials and tribulations of the world would be all over when one got to heaven."[19] Although Mays would advocate a more activist vision of ministerial leadership within the Black Church tradition, he often stated that he understood the great need for sermonic messages that somehow tried to mitigate the ravages of white supremacy for Black men, women, and children. As Mays contended, "Beaten down at every turn by the white man, as they were, Negroes could perhaps not have survived without this kind of religion."[20]

But in spite of the ability of such sermons to assuage Black people's pain, ministers like Reverend Marshall never developed a language to challenge white supremacy in any direct fashion. With a deeper understanding of what the writer Richard Wright called "the ethics of Jim Crow," Black preachers readily understood that each and every comment about racism and prejudice might invite some form of retaliation or even lynching.[21] For example, when a visiting minister came to Marshall's church and began to criticize white people from the pulpit, Marshall stopped the guest speaker at once. In spite of this being the period that African American religious historian Gayraud Wilmore described as the deradicalization of the Black Church, many whites still viewed Black religious gatherings as a threatening prospect that might inspire Black Christians to protest against the mounting indignities and injustices of Southern life during the era of Jim and Jane Crow segregation.[22] The sustained reluctance of many Black ministers of the early twentieth century to advocate serious progress in race relations remained largely invisible to the collective white imagination. As a result, some Black ministers were assaulted and killed while numerous Black churches were burned with tragic regularity during the late 1800s and early 1900s. Like their white counterparts, Black ministers often stressed middle-class values to their congregations while suggesting that many Black people found themselves in "shameful situations because of their sinful ways."[23] Rather than offering substantial condemnation of racial prejudice in American society, many pastors preferred to urge their congregants to improve their personal conduct and hygiene as a means of avoiding further rebukes from whites.

However, not all religious leaders in the African American community were afraid to tackle the volatile issue of white supremacy. In fact, some church leaders defiantly insisted that African Americans demand their rights. A prime example of this radical thread within the Black Church is AME Bishop Henry McNeal Turner who consistently spoke out on racial matters in the United States. Without question, Turner must be recognized as one of the most visionary and militant Black religious leaders of the late nineteenth and early twentieth centuries.[24] Having grown up in South Carolina as a free Black in the midst of slavery, Turner eventually became a US Army chaplain during the Civil War and later became a member of the Georgia House of Representatives during Reconstruction. In 1883, after the US Supreme Court declared the Civil Rights Act of 1875 unconstitutional, Turner called the US Constitution "a dirty rag, a cheat, a libel and ought to be spit upon by every Negro in the land."[25]

As fiery as his attack on American politics was at the time, Turner made an even more intense and significant impact on the African American religious experience. Once he joined the AME Church in the 1850s, Turner became very influential in the recruitment of new converts to Methodism, the proliferation of AME churches, and the mentoring of new church clergy throughout the South after the Civil War. He eventually became a bishop in the AME Church in 1880. Contrary to the dominant opinion in the AME Church largely outlined by the erudite Bishop Daniel Payne, his mentor, Turner became an outspoken supporter of controversial issues such as women's suffrage, opposition to US imperialism, the ordination of women ministers, and the Back-to-Africa movement. More important, he demonstrated little patience for anyone who considered Christianity a white man's religion. As he boldly yet simply asserted that "God is a Negro," he assaulted those who "believe God is a white-skinned, blue-eyed, straight-haired, projecting-nosed, compressed-lipped, and finely-robed white gentleman" as being completely foolhardy.[26] Turner's provocative "God is a Negro" thesis has given generations of preachers as well as scholars of the Black Christian tradition the foundation of a new theological vision that began to delve more meaningfully into the religious experience of African Americans.

Anna Julia Cooper's *A Voice from the South: By a Woman from the South* (1892) called for civil rights and woman's rights, serving as one of the first articulations of Black feminism.[27] The book advanced a vision of self-determination through education and social advancement for African American women. Written during her years as a teacher and principal at M Street High School in Washington, DC, the book's central thesis envisions Black women as God's divine instruments of racial redemption and social transformation. Even so, her entire perspective is predicated upon a Black-skinned Victorianism that, ironically, creates a dark corollary to the "cult of true womanhood."[28] She contends that the inherently violent nature of men contradicts the implicit goals of Western civilization so often that the only way to improve the general standing of both church and state is to foster the intellectual and spiritual development of Black women, because only they will bolster the well-being of Black families as well as the entire African American community. Taken further, Cooper advanced the view that it was the duty of educated and successful black women to support their less privileged contemporaries in achieving their goals.

During the early decades of the twentieth century, a majority of African Americans belonged to one of the historically Black Baptist or Methodist churches. As educator and civil rights leader Booker T. Washington observed, "If a Black man is anything but a Baptist or Methodist, someone has been tampering with his religion."[29] That comment notwithstanding, there were many Black women, men, and children by the start of the twentieth century who belonged to other churches and denominations besides the Baptists and Methodists— or occasionally belonged to no organized religion at all. For example, most African Americans identified Black Episcopalians with wealth and privilege, whether this generalization was made fairly or not. Many of those Black Episcopalians, however, traced their heritage to free Black families in the United States prior to the Civil War. By 1903, there were approximately fifteen thousand Episcopalian worshipers in various urban communities in the North and South, most notably Charleston, Raleigh, and Richmond.

The historic Black Church tradition helped hundreds of thousands of African American newcomers adapt to the challenges of urban life during the Great Migration, the gradual movement of five hundred thousand African Americans from the South to northern and midwestern cities from 1915 to 1921 in search of new job opportunities and better living conditions.[30] Yet the relationship between the Black religious tradition and the everyday lives of African Americans was always in flux. For instance, the growing popularity of the blues and jazz, being performed in nightclubs during the 1920s, was gradually being integrated into urban gospel music.[31] Many nightclub musicians and singers received their training and made their first public performance in their home churches.

THE AZUSA STREET REVIVALS
AND THE RISE OF BLACK PENTECOSTALISM

Undeniably, the most significant growth within the Black Church tradition was the Holiness and Pentecostal movements. The Holiness movement and the advent of the Pentecostal church movement greatly affected Baptist and Methodist congregations. Partly in reaction to the elite domination and stiff authority of white Methodism, the Holiness movement gained a foothold among white people and then spilled over among Black Southerners. Holiness churches ordained women such as Neely Terry to lead them. Holiness clergy preached the Wesleyan notion of sanctification, an ideal that allowed a Christian to receive a "second blessing" and to feel the "perfect love of Christ" through the anointing of the Holy Spirit. Believers thus achieved an emotional reaffirmation and a new state of grace.

The Church of God in Christ (more commonly known as COGIC) became the leading Black Holiness church. The roots of this movement can be traced to a series of successful revivals in Mississippi and Memphis. Charles Harrison Mason and Charles P. Jones—two Black former Baptists—cofounded the COGIC church in 1907. However, C. H. Mason was expelled from the movement after reporting that "a flame touched [his] tongue" and that his "language changed." In other words, Mason had announced that he received the spiritual gift of *glossolalia* (speaking in tongues).

After leaving the COGIC church, Mason proceeded to organize the Pentecostal General Assembly of the Church of God in Christ, and he assigned several Black men to serve as bishops in Mississippi, Arkansas, Texas, Missouri, and California. In 1911, Mason appointed Lizzee Woods Roberson to lead the Woman's Department, a post she held until 1945. She transformed that department into a financial powerhouse for COGIC. William J. Seymour also played a key role in the development of the new church. After hearing Black people speak in tongues in Houston, Seymour went to the Azusa Street revivals in Los Angeles in 1906. It was during this historic gathering that he and others also began to speak in tongues. There he founded the highly evangelistic church that shortly became the Pentecostal Church. Claiming the name of the movement from the story of Pentecost found in Acts of the Apostles chapter 2, the movement attracted enormous interest from churchgoers of all races and grew rapidly.

Bishop C. H. Mason joined the Pentecostal movement and, under his leadership, the Reorganized Church of God in Christ became the leading Pentecostal denomination; Mason remained presiding bishop until his death in 1961. Reverend James O. Patterson Sr. was made a COGIC bishop by Mason in 1953 and later became the presiding bishop in 1968. During his twenty-one-year tenure, Bishop Patterson vastly expanded the scope of the COGIC denomination by building the church's first seminary, Charles Harrison Mason Theological Seminary, as a part of the Interdenominational Theological Center in Atlanta, Georgia, as well as a publishing house and numerous other businesses. Another symbol of the COGIC's legacy is Mason Temple in Memphis, Tennessee, which serves as the denominational headquarters.

The permanence of the Holiness tradition was soon established as the COGIC movement spread across the South among Black and white people. Though there were racial tensions between Black and white believers especially in the South, the Pentecostal Church was the only movement of any significance within the historic Black Church tradition that crossed the proverbial color line in American society. The burgeoning growth of the COGIC movement was especially unique because it had moved from its roots in Afro-Protestantism to gain members and influence as a multiracial, multicultural, and multiethnic church movement. More notable than the rapid growth of the Holiness movement within the African American religious experience is the fact that COGIC church rejected any prospect for a theology or church ministry that was socially engaged. In spite of the various internal divisions that began to emerge within the historic Black Church traditions such as elitism, denominationalism, and secularism, COGIC and the larger Pentecostal movement have had an inexorable impact on the development of Black Christianity in the contemporary United States by promoting a theological doctrine that emphasized a strict interpretation of the gospel, energetic worship experience, sanctification, and the divine gift of speaking in tongues.[32]

THE BLACK CHURCH AND THE EMERGENCE OF THE CIVIL RIGHTS MOVEMENT

Unquestionably, the modern civil rights movement was the most important social protest movement of the twentieth century, and it would have been impossible without the historic Black Church tradition. Typically the civil rights movement refers to a set of significant events and reform movements aimed at abolishing public and private acts of racial discrimination against African Americans from 1954 to 1968, focusing particularly on the Deep South region of the United States. The objectives of the civil rights movement were intended to provide racial dignity, economic and political self-sufficiency, and freedom from white supremacy; but the centrality of African American theological and ethical perspectives was vital to Black people. At that time, Blacks, who were locked out of the formal political process due to racial barriers, were able to mount numerous campaigns over three decades to eradicate racial injustice and, in the process, transform the nation. Grounded in the social teachings of the Black Church tradition, the greatest accomplishment of the civil rights movement was that it successfully eliminated the American apartheid system of Jim and Jane Crow.[33]

Before Rev. Dr. Martin Luther King Jr.'s arrival to Dexter Avenue Baptist Church in Montgomery, Alabama, in the early 1950s, Rev. Vernon Johns was the church's pastor. Reverend Johns was a renowned and stirring preacher in his own right. During his tenure, Reverend Johns raised the banner of social justice in a town very uncomfortable with such activism, and his unwavering stance on civil rights and human dignity often proved too provocative for him to remain pastor of the city's most elite African American congregation. In the heart of the fundamentalist and racist South, Johns often based his sermons on biblical texts that illuminated the hypocrisy of white Christians as they also bolstered a sense of racial pride for Black Christians. Moreover, he frequently challenged his own Black middle-class congregation to follow the teachings of Jesus more explicitly by eschewing materialism and individualism in favor of heightened levels of social responsibility as well as racial solidarity. Having grown tired of their pastor's sharp social commentary and unrelenting tongue, the members of Dexter Avenue eventually pressured Reverend Johns to resign his pastorate.[34]

Black Youth, Black Churches, and Early Civil Rights Struggle

Without a doubt, *Brown v. Board of Education of Topeka* was a landmark decision of the United States Supreme Court that explicitly outlawed racial segregation of public schools, ruling so on the grounds that the doctrine of "separate but equal" public education could never truly provide black Americans with facilities of the same standards available to white Americans. For much of the ninety years prior to 1954, race relations in the United States had been dominated by Jim and Jane Crow segregation, particularly, but not exclusively, in the American South. Under the visionary legal strategy of Thurgood Marshall and the National Association for the Advancement of Colored People (NAACP) legal defense team, the plaintiffs in *Brown v. Board of Education* asserted that the system of racial separation, while masquerading as providing separate but equal treatment of both white and Black Americans, instead perpetuated inferior accommodations, services, and treatment for Black Americans.[35] On May 17, 1954, the Warren Court handed down a unanimous decision stating, in no uncertain terms, that "separate educational facilities are inherently unequal." Despite this momentous ruling, not everyone readily accepted the Brown decision, a point made obvious by the "Massive Resistance" organized throughout the Deep South in rebellion to the desegregation ruling from the US Supreme Court.[36]

Too often, when we talk about history in general and especially the civil rights movement, we tend to focus on the great figures and famous names at the top of society without paying enough attention to the ordinary folks that our traditional approaches to history tend to overlook. Paying attention to ordinary people is especially important in the civil rights struggle because it should always be seen as a grassroots movement. The daily fight for freedom, justice, equality, and human dignity is not just about one great person in history but about a united effort of each and every individual willing to put himself or herself at risk for the chance to live to his or her fullest potential. Throughout the history of the civil rights movement, young people were crucial to making the struggle for freedom, justice, and equality a reality. Here are some examples of how some key young women and men helped create the context for Dr. King's eventual leadership of the civil rights movement. The most traditional starting point in the history of the civil rights movement is the *Brown vs. Board of Education* Supreme Court decision in 1954. But overwhelming attention is given to Thurgood Marshall and the NAACP lawyers as well as to Chief Justice Earl Warren's leadership of the US Supreme Court. However, when we reconsider the story of the Brown case from the perspectives of the children and their families, you see something totally different. The story of how racial segregation was ended in America could just as easily begin with Rev. Oliver L. Brown and his daughter, Linda.[37] At the time, Linda was a third grader who had to walk six blocks to her school bus stop in order to ride to Monroe Elementary, her segregated Black school, which was one mile away, while Sumner Elementary, an all-white school, was no more than seven blocks from her house. As directed by the NAACP leadership, the neighborhood parents attempted to enroll their children in the closest neighborhood school in the fall of 1951. Of course, because of the dominance of Jim and Jane Crow segregation, they were refused enrollment and directed to the segregated schools.

Brown had initially contacted a Topeka attorney about his concerns regarding "separate but equal" policies of the schools in his city. In turn, the lawyer referred Brown to the local NAACP chapter in Topeka. In the words of the famous Black novelist Richard Wright, the Brown family, like countless other families of color, had to live according to the twisted and hateful "ethics of Jim Crow." Faced with the pain of having to teach self-hate, shame, and second-class citizenship to his child, Mr. Brown decided to do something to break the cycle. That bold step forward eventually allowed the possibility for the Little Rock Nine to integrate Central High School in 1957 and James Meredith to break the collegiate color barrier at the University of Mississippi a few years later. Whether in kindergarten or in college, the Black students who followed in Linda Brown's footsteps represent tens of thousands of young Black women and men who finally gained greater access to American education. Once alerted to the grave injustice of racial segregation, many college students across racial backgrounds organized into freedom rides and sit-ins during the early 1960s. Such brave and brilliant demonstrations of grassroots activism erupted primarily in the South, intent upon ending racial segregation in every corner of this nation.

Another key episode of the civil rights movement was the tragic fate of Emmett Till. Emmett was the son of Mamie and Louis Till. Mamie Till Bradley and Louis Till had separated in 1942. Emmett's father was drafted into the US Army in 1943 and died overseas two years later. As happens too often in our community, Emmett's mother largely raised him as a single parent. In 1955, Till and his cousin were sent for a summer stay with Till's great-uncle, who lived in Money, Mississippi, a small town in the Mississippi Delta. Before his departure, Till's mother cautioned him to "mind his manners" especially with white Southerners. Mamie Till knew that race relations in Mississippi were very different from those in Chicago, and she was fully aware of the long history of lynchings and racially motivated murders, especially in the region where Till was going to visit. She was mindful that there were news reports about increased racial tensions in the South after the United States Supreme Court's 1954 *Brown* decision to end segregation in public education. Above all, like so many Black families, Mrs. Till knew the risks; but she believed that, in spite of racist terror, her young son, Emmett, deserved to have a happy childhood in the company of other Black men of all ages who would help him grow into his own manhood.

Till arrived in Money, Mississippi, on August 21, 1955. Three days later, he joined other teenagers as they went to Bryant's Grocery and Meat Market to get some candy and soda. Till, his cousin, and several other black young men were all under the age of sixteen. Roy and Carolyn Bryant owned the market that catered mostly to the local sharecropper population. While standing in the store, Till showed his buddies some photos of his life back home, including one of him with his friends, including a white girl. The boys dared him to talk to a white woman in the shop. As Till was leaving the store, he allegedly said, "Bye, baby," to Carolyn Bryant. Taking immediate offense at his comment, she got up and stormed out to her car. The boys became terrified and ran for their lives. A few days later, upon his return to town from a road trip, her husband was greatly angered when he heard about the incident. Bryant and his half-brother, J. W. Milam, met late Sunday night to go and "teach the boy a lesson." On August 27, 1955, Bryant and Milam kidnapped Emmett Till from his great-uncle's house in the middle of the night. According to witnesses, they drove him in a car with two unknown people to a weathered shed on a plantation in a neighboring county. It was there that they brutally beat young Emmett before they fatally shot him. They then tied a cotton gin fan around his neck with some barbed wire to weigh down his broken body as they dropped it into the nearby Tallahatchie River. Although Bryant and Milam were eventually caught, arrested, and tried for Till's murder, the judge and all-white, all-male jury ignored the evidence and eyewitness testimony, and the men were acquitted. Based on the evidence, the white townsfolk believed the two men had every right to put young Emmett Till in his place, up to and including murdering him. The two men were paid $4,000 for an interview in *Look* magazine a year later. They did not fear being tried for the same crime again because of the constitutional protection against double jeopardy.

These grown men were offended by this teenager, believing that Emmett Till deserved to die for the supreme offense of "acting mannish," as we used to say back home. His mother had to cry those heartbreaking tears that no parent should ever have to shed for a child who died a cruel and untimely death. But, hard as this story is, this is symptomatic of a larger dilemma of how little worth the lives of Black people held in society at that time.

When Till's body was discovered, local authorities put his remains into a pine box for a simple burial, but Mamie Till wanted his body shipped back home to Chicago. A Tutwiler mortuary assistant worked all night to prepare the horribly disfigured body as best he could, so that Mamie Till could claim Emmett's body once it arrived in Chicago. The Chicago funeral home had promised not to open the casket, but Mamie Till fought it. After the state of Mississippi forbade the funeral home to open the casket, Mamie threatened to open it herself, insisting she had a right to see her son. After viewing the body, she insisted on leaving the casket open during the funeral. Furthermore, she allowed people to take photos because she wanted the whole world to see how badly Till's body had been disfigured. Photographs of Till's mutilated corpse circulated around the country, notably appearing in *Jet* magazine, and drew intense public reaction. Some reports indicate nearly fifty thousand people viewed the body while millions more saw the terrifying images in the news. The nation could not go back to business as usual in light of such horror perpetrated on helpless children. As a society, there are moments of crisis when we can no longer ignore the rising tide of death and violence when it affects our youngest and most precious members of society. To combat this pathological downward spiral, it is necessary to recognize that every person is a child of God worthy of being esteemed.

One person who saw Till's funeral photo and was moved to do something to fight the system was Rosa Parks. She was a seamstress by profession and secretary for the Montgomery, Alabama, chapter of the NAACP. The Montgomery bus boycott was triggered by her arrest on December 1, 1955, when she was charged for violating racial segregation laws in that city after refusing to give up her bus seat to a white man. As a result of her courage, Rosa Parks is considered one of the pioneers of the civil rights movement. E. D. Nixon, president of the Montgomery chapter of the NAACP and a labor organizer, planned the boycott before Rosa Parks's arrest. Nixon intended that her arrest be a test case to allow Montgomery's Black citizens to challenge segregation on the city's public buses. With this goal, community leaders had been waiting for the "right person" to be arrested, a person whose arrest would anger the Black community and prod it into action— someone who would agree to test the segregation laws in court, and who, most important, was "above reproach."

On March 2, 1955, Claudette Colvin, a fifteen-year-old student at Booker T. Washington High School boarded a public bus at the same place Parks boarded another bus months later. Colvin was sitting about two seats from the emergency exit when four whites boarded. The bus driver ordered four black passengers, including Colvin, to get up, and she refused. Shortly thereafter, she was handcuffed, arrested, and forcibly removed from the bus by two police officers, who took her to jail on assault charges. "The bus was getting crowded and I remember [the bus driver] looking through the rear view mirror asking her to get up out of her seat, which she didn't," Annie Larkins Price, a classmate of Colvin's at the time, testified on Colvin's behalf in the juvenile court case, where Colvin was convicted of violating the segregation law and assault. Price stated that Colvin "didn't say anything. She just continued looking out the window. She decided on that day that she wasn't going to move."[38]

After Colvin's father posted her bail, Nixon vowed to help the young woman battle this injustice. But the other leaders of the local NAACP began second-guessing the matter almost immediately. They argued that Colvin lived in the poorest section of Montgomery and came from a humble background in which her father mowed lawns and her mother was a maid. Moreover, the arresting police officers accused the teenager of spewing curse words as they took her to the city hall and then jail. Colvin denied it, saying that, in fact, the obscenities were being leveled at her. As the police took her away, Colvin did scream that her constitutional rights were being violated. No one on either the bus or the nearby sidewalk stopped to intervene on her behalf.

Despite the growing attacks on Colvin's reputation, a number of Montgomery's Black leaders, including Parks, raised money for her defense. At the time, Colvin was active in the NAACP's Youth Council, and she was actually being advised by Rosa Parks. Soon after her arrest, however, Colvin became pregnant by a much older, married man. Upon hearing this news, many local Black pastors and civic leaders felt that this moral transgression would embarrass the deeply religious Black community. They also felt this news made Colvin appear scandalous and suspicious even in the eyes of sympathetic whites. In particular, they knew that the white press would manipulate Colvin's pregnancy as a means of impugning her personal character and under-mining her victim status, thus making their attempts to protest the bus company meaningless. She was ultimately sentenced to probation for the ordinance violation, but a boycott and legal case never materialized from the event. One might argue that civil rights leaders, who were predominantly male and middle class, felt uneasy about defending Colvin's rights in light of her impoverished background and her status as an unmarried pregnant teen. As a matter of fact, even before Clau-dette Colvin and Rosa Parks, the NAACP had rejected several other Black victims they deemed unsuitable or unable to withstand the pres-sures of cross-examination during a legal challenge to racial segregation laws for similar reasons. E. D. Nixon later explained, "I had to be sure that I had somebody I could win with."[39] Ultimately, Parks was a good candidate because of her good standing in the community.

After Rosa Parks refused to comply with the Jim Crow law that required her to give up her seat on a public bus to a white man on De-cember 1, 1955, members of the Montgomery Improvement Associa-tion and the NAACP worked in conjunction with local Black churches willing to support Parks's fight against the city ordinance. As a result, the Montgomery bus boycott began on December 5, 1955, in Mont-gomery, Alabama. It was intended to oppose the city's policy of racial segregation on its public transit system. The ensuing struggle lasted until December 21, 1956, (roughly 386 days) and not only resulted in a US Supreme Court decision that declared the local and state laws requiring segregated buses unconstitutional but also inspired the emer-gence of the modern civil rights movement under the leadership of Dr. Martin Luther King Jr.[40]

In between Parks's arrest and trial dates, a meeting of local Black ministers was hosted at the Dexter Avenue Baptist Church, where Dr. King was pastor. After the Montgomery Improvement Association (MIA) was established, the group proposed a list of demands to present to the city's leaders and selected Dr. King to lead the boycott. King was initially chosen to lead the boycott because the young minister was new to Montgomery, and the city leaders had not had time to intimidate him. Later, at another, larger gathering of ministers, the MIA's agenda was threatened by the reluctance of most Black clergy to support the campaign. Nixon was incensed and threatened to reveal the ministers' cowardice to the Black community. In the midst of this potential chaos, Dr. King spoke up, declaring that he was not afraid to support the boycott. Not only did King demonstrate that he had the courage to lead the MIA, but he also snatched victory from the jaws of almost certain defeat by keeping the clergy and activists united by their common cause. With the successful resolution of the Montgomery bus boycott of 1955–56 as well as the evolution of the Greensboro sit-in desegregation movement in 1960, a new cadre of political leaders such as Ralph Abernathy, Ella Baker, Roy Innis, James Bevel, John Lewis, James Lawson, Andrew Young, Fred Shuttlesworth, and other notable figures arose to the upper echelons of the nation's civil rights organizations.[41]

Black Religious Leadership and the Civil Rights Movement

Without question, the two most chronicled leaders of the civil rights era have been Martin Luther King Jr. and Malcolm X. Although both men are generally represented as polar opposites on issues such as interracial coalitions, nonviolent civil disobedience, and other issues, Martin Luther King Jr. and Malcolm X found common ground in terms of their mutual commitment to the Black freedom struggle. In his comparative study of Martin and Malcolm, James Cone contends that both of these historic figures sought to overturn prevailing systems of domination and oppression by empowering the downtrodden in the United States and worldwide in their respective ways.[42] On the one hand, Malcolm X's life was characterized by constant transformation from his marginal existence as a ghetto hustler to national spokesperson for the Nation of Islam to foremost Black nationalist of his generation to the preeminent advocate of Black Power and Third World liberation movements. Because Malcolm X's radical outlook and controversial statements were frequently subject to misinterpretation and gross distortion by critics and admirers alike, it is crucial to examine his historical context as well as the content of his uncompromising political commentary. With the resurgence of African American consciousness and identity associated with the Black Power era of the late 1960s, many Blacks elevated Malcolm X to the level of sociopolitical and cultural icon capable of great personal and intellectual transformations.[43]

On the other hand, the literature on the life and legacy of Dr. King as both a national hero and one of the country's most influential public theologians is already expansive in nature.[44] For instance, there is a general tendency to reduce King's prophetic witness and critical intellect to what he learned from the Black Church tradition during his childhood. Arguably, this oversimplified concept of King's theological and intellectual development can be attributed to the pioneering African American religious scholar Joseph Washington, who states that King was "a remarkable product of the South; barely tainted by his academic exposure in the North."[45] Whereas Washington's perspective is not incorrect, it is definitely incomplete. In like fashion, historian August Meier ostensibly downplays the intellectual merits of King's speeches and writings as being rather "eclectic" and "superficial," a mélange of thoughts that seem incongruous and irreconcilable in nature. In spite of such a harsh condemnation of King's intellectual output, Meier— ever the meticulous researcher—does manage to identify the essence of King's intellectual corpus in good form.[46]

However, such disregard for the profound nature of King's intellectual and spiritual trajectory is dismissive of the entire documentary record that he has left behind for scholars, as evidenced by historian Clayborne Carson's herculean efforts to organize and distill Dr. King's personal and professional papers. Viewing King in this fashion might extol the virtues and values derived from King's formative years in the Black Baptist tradition, but such an outlook makes it far too easy to ignore the momentous effort on King's part to translate, transform, transcribe, and transcend his more staid thoughts about both church and society in ways that reflected his experiences as an educated adult from his undergraduate years at Morehouse College to his doctoral work at Boston University and beyond. Therefore, this arrested-development thesis surrounding King as a historical figure must be dismantled in order to overcome the presumed anti-intellectualism embedded within scholarly treatments of the historic Black Church tradition overall and the role of Black churches in the Southern civil rights movement in particular. In the hopes of promoting a more robust and meaningful treatment of King's intellectual contributions and religious leadership, there needs to be concerted effort to avoid oversimplification or eva-siveness of the complex, challenging, and even occasionally contradic-tory nature of King's thought and praxis for the sake of a more multi-dimensional narrative.

When grappling with the elements of the varying attributes of King's deep self-sacrificial commitment to the establishment of social justice and human equality, we must give serious consideration to the centrality of prophetic witness in King's contributions to civil rights leadership. Toward this end, scholars such as Lewis Baldwin, Robert Franklin, and Albert Raboteau have characterized the prophetic nature of King's thought in terms of his willingness to stand apart from the mainstream.[47] For example, envisioning King as part of this historic mission, Richard Lischer argues that Dr. King strove to carry the gos-pel of nonviolence, justice, redemption, and righteous rage in the face of suffering, which he preached from behind the pulpit of his father's Ebenezer Church in Atlanta, Georgia, "into world history."[48]

Following the overall success of the Montgomery bus boycott, Dr. King was instrumental in the founding of the Southern Christian Leadership Conference (SCLC) in 1957, a group created to harness the moral authority and organizing power of Black churches to con-duct nonviolent protests in the service of civil rights reform. Dr. King continued to dominate the organization until his death.[49] The SCLC derived its membership principally from Black communities associated with Baptist churches. Dr. King was an adherent of the philosophies of nonviolent civil disobedience used in India's decolonization struggle against the British by Mahatma Gandhi. In turn, Dr. King applied this Gandhian philosophy of *satyagraha* to the protests organized by the SCLC.[50] The organization's nonviolent principles were criticized by some Blacks and later challenged by the Student Nonviolent Coordi-nating Committee (SNCC).[51]

Dr. King and the SCLC applied the principles of nonviolent direct action with a series of victories by strategically choosing the timing, lo-cation, and methods in which the protests were conducted, often insti-gating dramatic standoffs with segregationist local authorities.[52] Some-times, these staged confrontations between the marchers and the local authorities turned violent when pro-segregation supporters mobilized resistance as in Albany, Georgia; Birmingham, Alabama; St. Augustine, Florida; and Selma, Alabama. During the early 1960s, the group was considered more radical than the older NAACP yet more conservative than the younger SNCC. Notably, the SCLC had a mentoring relationship with the SNCC in its earlier years. However, the SNCC abandoned its nonviolent strategy by 1966 in favor of greater militancy. Much thought went into the naming of the Southern Christian Leadership Conference. The leadership of this civil rights organization wanted to attract attention from both African American and white people, without mentioning the name of any race, which would distance themselves from other races. More than that, the group's founders felt that the term *Christian* could be related to all Christians across the nation and reduce their critics' suspicions about their morality or politics.

As the leader of the SCLC, Dr. King headed one of the six most influential civil rights organizations of the twentieth century. Under the leadership of A. Philip Randolph of the Brotherhood of Sleeping Car Porters and working in conjunction with Roy Wilkins of the NAACP, Whitney Young Jr. of the National Urban League, James Farmer of the Congress of Racial Equality (CORE), and John Lewis of the SNCC, King and the SCLC were part of the coalition instrumental in coordinating the March on Washington for Jobs and Freedom in 1963. Originally conceived as a public event to dramatize the desperate condition of Blacks in the South, the organizers of the march intended to criticize and then challenge the federal government for its utter failure to uphold the constitutional rights of Blacks as well as its failure to protect the lives of civil rights workers across the South. However, the group yielded to pressure and influence from President John F. Kennedy, and the gathering ultimately took on a far less harsh tone than originally imagined. The march did, however, seek very specific demands: an end to racial segregation in public education; meaningful civil rights legislation, including a law prohibiting racial discrimination in employment; protection of civil rights workers from police brutality; an increased minimum wage for all workers; and self-government for the District of Columbia, then governed by a congressional committee.[53]

As we shift the focus toward the civil rights movement of the mid-twentieth century, it is important to note that the social crisis that was being confronted—Jim and Jane Crow segregation—demanded a mode of preaching that was resolutely committed to facing the problems of the world while pressing toward the promise of heaven. What too often seems to get lost in translation regarding the civil rights movement is how deeply tied the bulk of the movement was to establishing greater opportunities and life chances for future generations of all Americans but especially African Americans. When we think of the key flashpoints of the movement—the Brown decision, the murder of Emmett Till, the heroic stand of the Little Rock Nine, or the Children's March during the Battle of Birmingham to name only a few—we see countless instances when the nonviolent civil rights struggle transformed the needs of children into means by which to reclaim and ultimately expand democracy for everyone.

One great oversight in the movement's history is the realization of how young Dr. King was at the start of the civil rights movement. When he became the leader of the Montgomery bus boycott, Dr. King was twenty-six years old, which was incredibly young to lead a movement that eventually revolutionized the entire world. He was a recent newlywed, a father of an infant daughter, a newly minted PhD, a third-generation Black Baptist preacher, and the hotshot new pastor of the Dexter Avenue Baptist Church, the most upwardly mobile Black congregation in Montgomery. Following the tremendous success of the Montgomery bus boycott, Dr. King was imagining how to take the civil rights struggle even further. In his classic book *Why We Can't Wait*, Dr. King discusses how he and other civil rights leaders were attempting to bring national attention to the racial crisis in Birmingham, Alabama, in 1963.[54] They believed that the time was right for a mass civil rights demonstration. As they were planning, they ran into a substantial problem: they could not find enough adults to raise the numbers to make a big enough impact. However, Rev. James Bevel and other local organizers had been working with Black schoolchildren and teenagers throughout the city and knew that they would be willing to hit the streets if no adults were ready, willing, or able to do so.

Meanwhile, in the face of the Children's March, Bull Connor, the racist public safety commissioner of Birmingham, gave his police forces the order to crush the young Black protesters, resulting in some of the most horrifying images and unforgettable moments of the civil rights era. Those young Black people—too many to name—were using their constitutional rights of freedom of speech and freedom of assembly to petition this nation to give them a better, brighter future. They faced police brutality, tear gas, attack dogs, high-powered fire hoses, and widespread arrests by police officers who were sworn to torment and abuse rather than to protect and serve. When the smoke cleared on that fateful day, more than three thousand people were arrested, many of them Black children and teens. That infamous moment in American history known as the Battle of Birmingham would not have been possible without the hundreds, if not thousands, of young Blacks willing to put their precious lives and bodies in harm's way.

Moreover, thinking what was at stake for future generations of Black youth fueled many leaders to go further than they might have ever thought possible. For example, Rev. Dr. Martin Luther King Jr.'s "Letter from Birmingham City Jail" from April 1963 offers another prime example of prophetic witness that boldly bridges the gap between pastoral care and prophetic confrontation to those around him. Written secretly from the confines of a nondescript jail cell during Easter weekend in 1963, this letter is very much in keeping with the classic prophetic tradition of the Hebrew Bible because it confronts the keepers of the faith from within the faith while also challenging a faulty mode of social praxis that fails to live up to and into God's vision. This powerful jailhouse letter also stands in the fine legacy of the apostolic epistolary tradition by examining problems within the Christian faith community, offering insight, encouragement, and instruction for the long struggle ahead, while exhorting the call as well as the cost for true discipleship in a world of contrary conditions. At the heart of this legendary document, King offers what is the chief reason why the movement had to move forward with no thought of retreat: "We have waited for more than 340 years for our constitutional and God given rights."[55]

Shifting his focus ever so slightly, King takes direct aim against eight white clergy from mainline churches in Birmingham. After they condemned his leadership of the nonviolent struggle against Bull Connor's forces in the "Battle of Birmingham," King challenges the role and voice of the "liberal" Christian church in American society that chooses to remain silent in the face of widespread injustice and lethal violence perpetuated against their fellow Black citizens. For Dr. King, the church becomes not only impotent in such instances but also irrelevant when it serves as the quiet, uncritical sponsor of the status quo. King poses the necessary question: "Is organized religion too inextricably bound to the status quo to save our nation and the world?"[56]

Another key tension about the 1963 March on Washington arose concerning Dr. King's connection to Bayard Rustin. Rustin was an African American civil rights activist who counseled Dr. King in 1956 to devote himself wholeheartedly to the principles of nonviolence. However, Rustin's open homosexuality and his ties to the Communist Party USA caused many white and African American leaders to demand that Dr. King distance himself from Rustin, advice which he followed on several occasions. One occasion on which Dr. King did not surrender to such fears was when he welcomed Rustin's pivotal leadership role in organizing the 1963 March on Washington along with the movement's elder statesman, A. Philip Randolph.[57]

Despite tensions, the march was a resounding success. More than a quarter of a million people of diverse backgrounds were at the event, sprawling onto the National Mall and around the reflecting pool. At the time, it was the largest gathering of protesters in the history of the nation's capital. With live television coverage of the march, Dr. King's famous "I Have a Dream" speech from the steps of the Lincoln Memorial exhilarated the nation that day and has been regarded as one of the greatest speeches in American history. Largely due to the prominence garnered by popular reception of Dr. King's speech and its impact on the successful passage of civil rights legislation, Dr. King became the youngest recipient of the Nobel Peace Prize on October 14, 1964.

By the mid-1960s, there were two major issues that changed the trajectory of the civil rights movement: the Vietnam War and the quest for economic justice. As the prevailing visionary of the civil rights movement, Dr. King confronted both these concerns in profound ways during the last years of his life. Challenged by the carnage and corruption he witnessed in America's war in Vietnam, Dr. King expanded his appreciation of nonviolence as the core of the Christian way of life in global terms. On April 4, 1967, Dr. King delivered his "Beyond Vietnam" sermon at the Riverside Church in Harlem wherein he made a bold denunciation of American bloody and immoral military involvement in Southeast Asia.[58]

There were several reasons for Dr. King and other civil rights leaders to turn their attention to the issue of the Vietnam War as an urgent concern. First, the civil rights movement represented the moral conscience of the nation, and the Vietnam War quickly had become the moral crisis of a generation, so, as a Christian, Dr. King believed he had to bear witness against such an atrocity. Second, Dr. King was among the growing number of civil rights and antiwar activists who recognized that the billions of dollars spent on supporting and expanding the war could have been spent on improving American society. Third, for all citizens to have equal rights, the entire American society, including its foreign policy, needed to be redefined. Fourth, given the racial dimensions and racist attitudes incumbent within the Vietnam War, the war was especially within the purview of African American interests. Finally, speaking out against the war was a way of overcoming mainstream America's desire that Black people have presence without voice.[59] Dr. King also stated in his "Beyond Vietnam" sermon that, from Vietnam to South Africa to Latin America, the United States had positioned itself in direct opposition to the emergent spirit of revolutionary anti-imperialism among the vulnerable and impoverished people of the Third World, instead of supporting them in any worthwhile or meaningful fashion.

In 1968, Dr. King and the SCLC organized the "Poor People's Campaign" to address issues of economic justice. The campaign culminated in a march on Washington, DC, that demanded economic aid to the poorest communities of the United States. He crisscrossed the country to assemble a legion of poor Americans of all races that would descend on Washington—engaging in nonviolent civil disobedience at the Capitol, if need be—until Congress enacted a "Poor People's Bill of Rights." The proposed legislation called for a massive government jobs-training program in order to rebuild America's inner cities. He saw a crying need to confront Congress, which had demonstrated its antipathy towards the nation's poorest and most disadvantaged citizens by appropriating federal funding for the military at astronomical levels while downplaying the desperate needs for domestic social welfare programs.[60]

In March 1968, Rev. James Lawson invited Dr. King to Memphis, Tennessee, in order to garner greater support for a strike by local sanitation workers who had launched a campaign for union representation after two workers accidentally were killed on the job. On the night of April 3, 1968, struggling to overcome his own bout with illness and exhaustion, Dr. King spoke to a euphoric crowd at Mason Temple in Memphis, giving his famous "I've Been to the Mountaintop" speech in a fashion inspired by the Black Church tradition's deep-seated embrace of the Bible's prophetic imperative.[61] After roughly thirteen years of leading the Black freedom struggle in America, Dr. King was assassinated on April 4, 1968. That date has essentially come to symbolize the end of the civil rights movement for most scholars.

Spurred by Dr. King's murder, a series of violent uprisings broke out in over 110 cities, notably in Chicago, Baltimore, and Washington, DC. In the days that followed, Rev. Ralph Abernathy succeeded Dr. King as the head of the SCLC and attempted to carry forth Dr. King's intended plan for a massive "Poor People's March," which would have united poor people of all racial and ethnic backgrounds to demand fundamental changes in American social and economic structure. The march went forward under Abernathy's straightforward leadership but is widely regarded as a failure. By 1966, the emergence of the Black Power movement, which arguably lasted until 1975, enlarged and gradually eclipsed the civil rights movement in its focus on Black empowerment and community development but became more secular in its orientation.[62] Despite this turn of events, it was through coordinated, cooperative efforts among Black clergy and laity at the national and local levels that any lasting victories toward implementing the "Beloved Community" envisioned by Dr. King have been achieved thus far.[63]

A major reason for the civil rights movement's success was its religious leadership. Although Rev. Dr. Martin Luther King Jr. is probably the most celebrated and best-known African American religious leader in American history, Black activist ministers such as Ralph Abernathy, Fred Shuttlesworth, Adam Clayton Powell Jr., C. T. Vivian, Wyatt T. Walker, Prathia Hall, Kelly Miller Smith Sr., James Bevel, Gardner C. Taylor, Joseph Lowery, Andrew J. Young, and Leon H. Sullivan were just a handful of the gifted religious figures who played leadership roles at both the local and national levels during the height of the civil rights movement. In many instances, Black clergy became the designated spokespeople for campaigns articulating the grievances of Black people, and they also became the chief strategists who shaped the objectives and methods of the movement that sought to redress those grievances. Furthermore, they were able to win the allegiance of a large number of people and convince them to make great sacrifices for racial justice.

One attribute that helped Black ministers gain support for the civil rights struggle was their charismatic Black preaching style. As homiletics expert Henry Mitchell illustrates, the power of Black preaching was used both to convey meaning and to inspire people involved in the struggle for racial equality.[64] The sacred rhetoric used by these Black activist ministers explained that the civil rights activists were engaged in a religious as well as a historic mission. Many of the Black preachers spoke of the "holy crusade" to force America to live up to its promise of democracy. For example, in a 1963 campaign to force the state of New York and the construction unions to hire Black and Hispanic workers, Rev. Gardner C. Taylor, the pastor of Concord Baptist Church in Brooklyn, declared to a crowd of six thousand, "There will be no turning back until people in high places correct the wrongs of the nation."[65] Presumed to be moral leaders of the African American community, ministers like Taylor were able to use rhetoric gifts such as imagery, verbal quickness, rhythmic cadence, and reiteration in their sermons and speeches that evoked an emotional response from their audience. These performances convinced followers that their cause was right and that God called their pastors to a divine task. Many participants in the Montgomery bus boycott noted that they became involved in the campaign because their charismatic pastors inspired them. Moreover, as televisions soon became commonplace in tens of millions of American homes, eloquent ministers such as Dr. King soon became ubiquitous spokespeople for the Black community as well as formative leaders of the Black freedom struggle thanks largely to the predominantly white mass media.

But the religious leadership of the civil rights movement was not limited solely to these ministers; it also encompassed lay church leaders and community activists, many of whom had still deeper roots in their local Black communities than the ministers. Besides nurturing charismatic Black male ministers, Black churches also helped instill and inspire key African American moral values in grassroots leaders, most of whom were women, by emphasizing the desire of freedom, justice, and equality at the core of Black Christian beliefs.[66] The cultivation of these spiritual and moral values usually took place outside of conventional, male-dominated avenues of ministerial training such as seminaries, ministerial alliances, and denominational conventions, which emphasized a hierarchical approach to leadership. Instead, the institutions responsible for inculcating cooperative as well as democratic values in church members—clubs, choirs, missionary societies, and other church auxiliaries—were both created and operated by lay leaders and members of churches.

In church auxiliaries, most of which were created and run by women of the church, members learned to handle money, speak in public, and work on behalf of the less fortunate. Auxiliaries provided a space in which members socialized, developed strong bonds, and worked on tasks in a supportive atmosphere. Although the role of lay leaders in the civil rights movement is still pretty much an unwritten history, there is evidence that auxiliaries played a pivotal role in what happened. For instance, the laity of Black churches organized the car-pools used during the bus boycotts in Louisiana and Alabama. Many of the civil rights workers, especially the young "Freedom Riders" and sit-in protesters during the early 1960s, willingly became "jailbirds for freedom," volunteering to be arrested as the ultimate expression of civil disobedience.[67] This willingness to make a sacrifice for the Black freedom struggle was encouraged by the collective sentiment fostered in these church auxiliaries. For instance, most of the Black women active in the Montgomery, Alabama, bus boycott belonged to Baptist churches and were members of those church choirs, missionary societies, usher boards, pastor aid societies, and other auxiliaries. Although many asserted that they became involved in the movement because of their pastors' leadership, others attributed their involvement to their belief in a religion that dedicated itself to confronting the social conditions of the oppressed in keeping with the biblical mandate that all Christians must care for "the least of these."[68]

The collective sentiment of helping the oppressed had been a long-standing objective of these lay religious organizations. Take, for example, Ella Baker, one of the movement's most unsung leaders and thinkers with her work in both the SCLC and the SNCC. In her work with the SCLC, Ms. Baker often clashed with Dr. Martin Luther King Jr. because she did not believe in the "one great leader" model of social change, striving instead to empower ordinary people by the thousands to speak out against social injustice. Baker later recalled her mother's involvement with the women's missionary movement of Black Baptist churches and how her mother embraced the missionary groups' emphasis on cooperative nature and communal spirit based in Christian scripture over and above the traditional folkways of Black Southerners. Those early childhood lessons in which she learned about mutual concern for oppressed individuals and communities greatly influenced Baker's thinking and political activism throughout her adult life. Furthermore, her radical and inclusive vision of democracy based on Black Christian social teachings enabled her to prepare an entire generation of young male and female activists, both black and white, to continue the collective quest for social justice.[69] As a tribute to her contributions, Ms. Baker's words and philosophy have been immortalized in Sweet Honey In The Rock's "Ella's Song (We Who Believe in Freedom Cannot Rest)" penned by singer-songwriter Bernice Johnson Reagon, a civil rights activist trained by Ms. Baker.

Another influential lay leader in the civil rights struggle who expressed the core values of the historic Black Church tradition was Fannie Lou Hamer. Born in poverty, Hamer finished only the sixth grade and picked cotton to survive in rural Mississippi during the height of Jim and Jane Crow segregation. Ms. Hamer professed that the Black Baptist church she attended was a central part of her life, shaping her reading and interpretation of the Bible. As a deeply religious woman,

Ms. Hamer proclaimed that religious convictions directly informed her politics. After she joined the SNCC, she dedicated herself to improving the lives of Black families.[70] Robert Moses, head of the Mississippi Freedom Summer Campaign, noted that Hamer sang the spirituals that she had learned in the church at civil rights gatherings to help foster a genuine feeling of community among the young SNCC activists. Hamer became field secretary for the SNCC and was later a founding member of the Mississippi Freedom Democratic Party (MFDP), and she ran for Congress. She helped lead the voter registration campaign in Mississippi and was arrested, beaten, and tortured for her activities.

Directly challenging the all-white Mississippi delegation to the Democratic National Convention in 1964, Ms. Hamer addressed the nation as leader of the MFDP in an infamous televised broadcast wherein she spoke of her own plight, the murder of civil rights activists, and the daily racist terror that Black Mississippians faced for attempting to exercise their rights as citizens. When President Lyndon B. Johnson and the Democratic Party's leadership, with the support of prominent civil rights leaders such as Dr. Martin Luther King Jr., worked out a compromise to give two seats to members of the MFDP, the group rejected the deal because all of the members would not be seated. It was Hamer who refused to compromise on the governing principles of the civil rights movement when she told the party leaders, "We didn't come for no two seats when all of us is tired."[71] In this and many other instances, she spoke truth to power in the spirit of the historic Black Church tradition in her willingness to question the nation's overall commitment to democracy for the disadvantaged members of society.

chapter 3

WE HAVE BEEN BELIEVERS
IN THE NEW JERUSALEM

The Black Church Tradition from Black
Liberation Theology to Barack Obama

Neither the slaves' whip nor the lynchers' rope nor the
bayonet could kill our black belief.

Margaret Walker, "We Have Been Believers"

As illustrated by the poem's title, Margaret Walker's "We Have Been Believers" is focused upon Black religious faith as a sustaining power for African Americans. During the latter half of the twentieth century, the United States witnessed sweeping changes in social, political, cultural, and economic realities that dramatically affected the spiritual lives and religious experiences of African Americans. More importantly, as Walker reminds us, preserving the core values and viewpoints of African American faith and culture in the face of horrific modes and trauma has been a crucial facet of the nation's history. Viewing religious faith as a bulwark for Black life and community in times past, the Black Church tradition has historically represented "a shelter in a time of storm." Similarly, Walker emphatically enjoins Black people to seize both the divine and the earthly power needed in order to bring forth spiritual, emotional, and political transformation in the future.

107

The enduring influence of the Black Church tradition is present throughout Walker's powerful poem even as she engages with Black religiosity in ways that are highly critical in order to incite greater levels of accountability and agency.[1] The era from the Black Power movement to the presidency of Barack Obama is defined by the advancement of African Americans toward greater levels of equality. Walker depicts this fulfillment of human flourishing as the eschatological concept of the "new Jerusalem." En route to witnessing the creation of the "new Jerusalem," there are several dynamic transformations from the end of the civil rights era that have posed great challenges in our strides toward equality as both a people and a nation.

SOCIAL DISLOCATION AND THE CHANGING FACE OF AMERICA'S FUTURE

The United States is currently undergoing the most profound demographic shift in its history. According to the 2010 US Census, white infants presently account for about 50 percent of total childbirths in the country. By 2030, the majority of US residents under eighteen will be persons of color. Moreover, Blacks, Latinos, Asians, Native Americans, Pacific Islanders, and other non-whites will collectively comprise the majority of the US population by 2042. For the first time since the founding of the American republic, the United States will be a "majority-minority" nation. In light of such a development, how will American society adjust to such historic demographic changes in its racial/ethnic composition over the next thirty to fifty years?

If we do not change course, we will continue on a path toward becoming a people and a nation defined by a spirit of divisiveness and rancor. For instance, it is estimated that a large portion of the rising non-white majority will remain unequal and insecure as long as the overwhelming share of the nation's wealth and power remains solidly in white hands. While it is anticipated that whites will make up a decreasing percentage of the American population through 2042 and beyond, wealthy white citizens will continue to control the lion's share of the nation's income and wealth.

But demographic predictions should never be confused with divine predestination, whether for better or worse. Faced with what sociologist Gunnar Myrdal called "America's original sin," communities of color have confronted the brunt of our nation's history of racism and white supremacy. Although there have been many socioeconomic and political gains made for all Americans over the past half-century, people of color continue to be at an extreme disadvantage in our society. Vast racial disparities still exist in wealth distribution, educational achievement, income potential, employment opportunities, home ownership, life expectancy, and other "quality of life" indicators.[2] Extreme inequality continues to further entrench racial disparities, which, in turn, threaten to shrink the Black middle class exponentially. This dilemma is compounded by mounting income disparities along racial lines that perpetuate poverty in communities of color in which the Black poverty rate will still be close to double that of whites. Such outrageous levels of increasing wealth inequality further entrenches the racial economic divide. The potential for racial and ethnic strife increases as larger numbers of people of color remain in poverty. The shift in numerical terms does not automatically dictate fair and equal treatment of all people in a manner reflecting God's plan for human dignity. Therefore, even as people of color become the new American majority, the persistent racial disparities of the past threaten to jeopardize the social fabric of our nation.

Education is one of the most important means for increasing social mobility and promoting positive cultural values, but persistent gaps in educational access and achievement along racial/ethnic lines are responsible for growing inequality for America's youth. By way of illustration, in 2010, Black adults were 60 percent as likely to have a college degree as their white counterparts. In addition to new restrictions on the use of race-based affirmative action in higher education, escalating college costs, the inadequate compensation of the nation's schoolteachers, and continued underfunding of public education in the United States threaten to reverse all the gains made since the 1960s.

This current educational crisis is coupled with the historically unprecedented mass incarceration of African Americans. By the most reasonable estimate, Blacks are six times more likely to be in prison than whites. Of the more than two million Americans currently housed in the nation's prisons, people of color will soon make up 65 percent of the US prison population. As one might imagine, this rising epidemic of incarceration has serious socioeconomic consequences. The devastating effects of incarceration haunt former inmates long after they have served their prison sentence. For example, an astonishing 68 percent of Black men born since the 1970s presently have prison records. Finding a job, purchasing a home, and pursuing an education is already difficult for anyone with a criminal record, but when that record is coupled with issues borne of racial inequality, the ex-prisoner's chance for a better life becomes nearly impossible.

Probably one of the greatest challenges to understanding this current historic era within the African American experience in terms of social dislocation arises from a larger shift within mainstream American society toward what is arguably called a "post-racial" outlook. Pulitzer Prize–winning journalist Eugene Robinson contends that, after decades of desegregation, affirmative action, immigration, and conservative social policies, the notion of Black America's solidarity has been altered forever. Robinson contends "There was a time when there were agreed-upon 'black leaders,' when there was a clear 'black agenda,' when we could talk confidently about 'the state of black America'—but not anymore."[3] The African American population in the United States has been seen perennially as a monolithic community—existing under the singular banner of "Black America"—with shared interests and unified needs. However, instead of talking about a unified Black America, Robinson contends that there are now five distinct subgroups: a significant but shrinking middle-class constituency with a full ownership stake in mainstream American society; an oversized underclass with less hope of escaping poverty and dysfunction than in any generation since the end of Reconstruction; a tiny albeit transcendent Black elite possessed of such vast wealth, remarkable clout, and enormous influence that the entire nation pays heed; individuals of biracial or mixed-race heritage who are trying to exist beyond the Black-white racial binary; and recent Black immigrants from across the African diaspora who have come to America by choice rather than by force.

The growing fragmentation of the assumed solidarity of racial identity in the contemporary era forces many of us to question what

"Black" is even supposed to mean. Robinson shows the various segments of Black America that are increasingly distinct and separated by demographic indicators, geographic location, and psychological outlook. They have strikingly different profiles, mind-sets, desires, fears, and dreams. What is more, these groups have become so disconnected from one another that they view one another with heightened envy, mistrust, doubt, and disdain. Yet, to make matters worse, all the respective parties are reluctant to acknowledge the divisions that create more barriers rather than bridges. Taken to its most logical extreme, the disintegration of a sense of cultural unity and racial solidarity advances a new paradigm for understanding Blackness in America, with implications that have proven both hopeful and disconcerting in ways that will endure for decades to come.

The final yet most important factor to this discussion is African American religious diversity in the contemporary era. The vast majority of African Americans are Protestant (78 percent), compared with only 51 percent of the US adult population as a whole. By a wide margin, African Americans stand out as the most Protestant racial/ethnic group in the United States when compared alongside whites (53 percent), Asians (27 percent), and Latinos (23 percent). But the current state of Protestantism in the United States and in the Black community is not homogeneous. Rather, it is divided into three distinct traditions: evangelical Protestant churches, mainline Protestant churches, and historically Black Protestant churches. More than 75 percent of African American Protestants (and 59 percent of African Americans overall) belong to historically Black Protestant denominations, such as the National Baptist Convention USA or the American Methodist Episcopal Church. In fact, 40 percent of all African Americans identify with Baptist denominations within the historic Black Church tradition. By several measures, including the perceived importance of religion in American life, attendance at religious worship services, and frequency of prayer and devotion, the historic Black Church denominations are among the most religiously observant faith communities. In fact, these and other measures suggest that members of historically Black Protestant churches tend to resemble the religious practices and beliefs held by white members of evangelical Protestant churches.

Beyond the parameters of the historic Black Church tradition, African Americans comprise 15 percent of evangelical denominations such as the Southern Baptist Convention or Assemblies of God. Additionally, African Americans represent 4 percent of mainline denominations, such as the United Church of Christ and the Disciples of Christ. Overall, the membership of historically Black Protestant denominations is 92 percent black, while African Americans make up relatively small portions of the membership of evangelical (6 percent) and mainline (2 percent) churches.

The most telling discovery of this survey data is that slightly more than 12 percent of African Americans identify themselves as having no particular religious affiliation. Although these "unchurched" individuals make up a smaller proportion of the African American community (12 percent) than the overall adult population (16 percent), the religiously unaffiliated actually constitute the third largest "religious" tradition within the Black community. However, very few African Americans (1 percent) describe themselves as either atheist or agnostic. Instead, most unaffiliated African Americans (11 percent of African Americans overall) simply describe their religion as "nothing in particular." Indeed, among the African American religiously unaffiliated populace, a significant majority (72 percent) says religion is at least "somewhat important" in their lives.[4] The shifting nature of the data surrounding the church's centrality within the African American experience is neither the only nor the most definitive way of gauging the significance of Black faith, but it is quite revelatory.[5]

BLACK POWER AND THE DEVELOPMENT OF NEW BLACK THEOLOGIES

Over the last four decades, there has been a tremendous change in African American Christianity in the United States and elsewhere around the world. The mood of many civil rights activists gradually became more militant in their outlook toward ending racial oppression and inequality. There was a general sense amongst a younger generation of Blacks that Dr. King and other leaders of the nonviolent phase of the Black freedom struggle were too moderate and therefore too willing to compromise with the white political establishment. In most regards, King was quite moderate among Black ministers. When it was first formed, the Student Nonviolent Coordinating Committee (SNCC) had been committed fully to nonviolent civil disobedience. Historian Clayborne Carson notes that the SNCC's early commitment to nonviolence waned greatly in later years once both leaders and rank-and-file members alike began to accept and condone violence in service of achieving justice. The passage of the Voting Rights Act of 1965 coincided with a week of deadly race riots in several cities across the country. While leading a voting rights march from Memphis, Tennessee, to Jackson, Mississippi, in the summer of 1966, James Meredith, the first African American student enrolled at the University of Mississippi in 1962, was shot and wounded. In response to this bloody, unprovoked attack, Stokely Carmichael and other younger leaders led protesters with clenched fists raised in the air while chanting "Black Power!" What was uttered as a catchy slogan during a protest march, "Black Power," quickly became recognized nationally as the symbol of a new spirit of Black militancy.[6]

For a growing number of Black Christians, chants of "Black Power" were increasingly embraced alongside talk of God's judgment upon America for the injustices done to Black people. By 1967, leaders of the National Committee of Negro Churchmen changed their group's name to the National Council of Black Churchmen (NCBC). The NCBC castigated mainstream white religious groups for their complicity with racism, demanded reparations, and agitated for substantive power or leadership roles within the governing structures of American society, both sacred and secular. In spring 1969, the NCBC hosted the Black Economic Development Conference (BEDC) in Detroit as a liberal community economic development.

Conventional wisdom amongst many Black leaders had long since recognized that economic freedom was one of the main keys to ending racial oppression so that American society could move beyond good intentions and toward meaningful transformation. At the BEDC gathering, Rev. James Forman and his fellow radical activists presented the "Black Manifesto," a document that demanded $500 million from white mainline Christian churches and Jewish synagogues as reparations that would offset the damage done by several centuries of political disenfranchisement and economic disadvantage. Moreover, Forman accused these faith communities of willing complicity and conscious participation with mainstream America's promulgation of slavery and segregation. This accusation was given further weight by calling out Christian and Jewish congregations for being slow to raise any complaints about Black oppression. It must be noted that the "Black Manifesto," as historian Robin D. G. Kelley observes, was "the first systematic, fully elaborated plan for reparations to emerge from the black freedom movement."[7]

Out of the interracial conflict and tension emerged various Black theologies that critiqued racism and other social injustices within modern society. Black liberation theology asserted the importance of conjoining religious practice and faith with political activism and social change for the betterment of the Black community. As one of the progenitors of Black liberation theology in terms of ministerial praxis, the Jaramogi Abebe Agyeman (Rev. Albert Cleage Jr.), pastor of Shrine of the Black Madonna (Pan African Orthodox Christian Church) in Detroit, Michigan, became a passionate advocate of Black Christian nationalism as defined in his books, *The Black Messiah* (1969) and *Black Christian Nationalism* (1972). In ways reminiscent of Henry McNeal Turner, Marcus Garvey, and Malcolm X, both Black liberation theology and Black Christian nationalism argued for the religious significance of envisioning Jesus Christ as a Black Messiah for the empowerment of Black Christians.

Without a doubt, the foremost leader in the development of Black liberation theology was theologian James H. Cone, whose early works include *Black Theology and Black Power* (1969), *A Black Theology of Liberation* (1970), *The Spirituals and the Blues: An Interpretation* (1972), and *God of the Oppressed* (1975). Cone's *Black Theology and Black Power* was the first academic treatise to merge the contemporaneous struggles for racial, political, and socioeconomic equality with the critical concerns of Christian systematic theology. By offering a forcefully prophetic call for a theology rooted in the Black experience, this pioneering work established Black liberation theology as an undeniable force within theological education and Black church praxis. A year later, Cone's *A Black Theology of Liberation* advanced this proposition by developing a theological outlook in which God identified with the oppressed in general and the historical plight of Black people struggling for freedom in the face of oppression in particular.

In the first work of African American systematic theology of liberation, *A Black Theology of Liberation* (1970), Cone framed his approach around the premise that "Christian theology is a theology of liberation. It is *a rational study of the being of God in the world in light of the existential situation of an oppressed community, relating the forces of liberation to the essence of the gospel, which is Jesus Christ.*"[8] In this fashion, Cone's first two volumes served as the foremost works of liberation theology written in the English language. Moreover, Cone's presupposition of the ontological Blackness of God coupled with divine identification with the Black oppressed illustrates the unwillingness of normative white theology to even consider its duty to help end oppression and injustice.

Although Cone was the first of the professional Black theologians to tackle the subject of liberation in a direct fashion, he was not alone in this endeavor. At various points, J. Deotis Roberts, Cecil Cone, Gayraud Wilmore, and William R. Jones were among a constellation of African American theologians and religious scholars who provided divergent visions of liberation in theological terms. For instance, Roberts offered a counterpoint to Cone's emphasis on liberation by juxtaposing it with concerns about reconciliation. According to Roberts, "liberation and reconciliation are the two main poles of Black Theology. They are not antithetical—one moves naturally from one to the other in the light of the Christian understanding of God and man."[9] Furthermore, he shares Cone's contention that

> freedom sums up what is. Liberation is revolutionary—for blacks it points to *what ought to be*. Black Christians desire radical and rapid social change in America as a matter of survival. Black Theology is a theology of liberation. We believe that the Christian faith is avowedly revolutionary and, therefore, it may speak to this need with great force.[10]

Thus, for Roberts, God's will at work in the world requires a concurrent commitment to liberating African Americans and reconciling them with white Americans. Much like Cone, Roberts also focused on race, but his emphasis was guided by concerns about mutuality and dialogue amongst equals. As such, Roberts not only effectively advances the prospect *for* liberation but also envisions reconciliation as the teleological goal *of* liberation in racial matters.

During the 1980s and 1990s, the pioneering works of Black theologians and religious scholars eventually gave rise to a new generation of self-identified Black intellectuals focused upon advancing the cause of liberation in a variety of new directions. In this fashion, the work of the second generation of Black male liberation theologians such as Josiah Young, James Evans, Noel Erskine, George Cummings, and Dwight Hopkins demonstrates the far-reaching possibilities of forging constructive Black theologies of liberation attentive to race, class, gender, and sexuality in both historical and global contexts.[11]

THE AWAKENING OF NEO-PENTECOSTALISM IN THE BLACK CHURCH TRADITION

In the wake of the historic Azusa Street revivals, there were various segments of the nascent Holiness and Pentecostal movements that wholeheartedly promoted a transcendent vision of sanctification that works beyond the boundaries of racial division. However, this lofty interracial vision soon collapsed as white Pentecostals broke away from their Black counterparts in order to organize their own churches along racial lines. Despite this rising tide of racial prejudice within Pentecostalism, countless Black Holiness and Pentecostal churches blossomed and flourished across the national landscape in an unfettered manner. Nevertheless, it was clear that, although racial segregation—both *de facto* (customary) and *de jure* (codified)—had been a prevalent aspect of American life throughout much of the twentieth century, the reintroduction of such blatant racism and bigotry was made explicit within a religious movement that had been interracial from its very inception.

In 1948, a founding membership consisting almost entirely of white congregations established the Pentecostal Fellowship of North America, an umbrella organization of Pentecostal (and later Charismatic) denominations. The same year also witnessed the origins of the nationwide salvation-healing crusades of prominent white evangelists, such as Billy Graham, Oral Roberts, and others, in which both Blacks and whites flocked together to the big tent revivals and worship services. In a bold step for this era, these white evangelists largely refused to establish racially segregated seating areas during their crusades. Therefore, even though the churches remained racially separate for quite some time, these crusades and big tent revivals provided opportunities for interracial worship amongst the Blacks and whites who flocked to these revivals.

By the 1990s, the racial climate had changed drastically in the United States. The civil rights movement and the subsequent legislative changes of the 1950s and 1960s had done a great deal to uproot the underpinnings of legalized segregation in American life. Regrettably, even as many doors of opportunity and advancement were opened for all to enter into the secular dimensions of American public life, the overwhelming majority of Pentecostal churches not only remained completely segregated but also were increasingly out of touch with the prospects for incorporating such changes. Recognizing that Pentecostalism's history of racial divisions needed to be brought to an end, church leaders from across the nation, under the leadership of Bishop Ithiel Clemmons of the Church of God in Christ (COGIC) and Bishop Bernard E. Underwood of the International Pentecostal Holiness Church, convened a special meeting in Memphis, Tennessee, on October 18, 1994. That evening, Rev. Donald Evans, a white pastor from the Gateway Christian Center Assembly of God in Tampa, Florida, attended the gathering in place of Assemblies of God pastor Mark Rutland, who missed the gathering because he had other responsibilities. The meetings reached a monumental climax when Evans ascended the dais with a basin of water and a towel. He tearfully explained that he felt God was leading him to wash the feet of Bishop Ithiel Clemmons. Evans later recalled,

I was surprised when I felt God's prompting to approach the platform and wash Bishop Clemmons' feet. But my simple response to God became like the proverbial rippling effect of a pebble in a pond. It amazes me how the Holy Spirit continues to speak through that small act of obedience.[12]

As Evans proceeded with the foot-washing ceremony, he apologized for the sins he and other whites had committed against their fellow Black Pentecostals gathered there and then begged for their forgiveness that evening as brothers and sisters in Christ. Awestruck by this unprecedented act, countless participants of both races openly wept in the auditorium's meeting hall that evening as they sensed that this beautifully grand gesture symbolized the Holy Spirit's approval over the proceedings. This event, which has become known as the "Memphis Miracle," marked a significant milestone regarding race relations within the history of Pentecostalism.

The Memphis Miracle of 1994 had a profound effect on Pentecostal church leaders. For example, many leaders in the Assemblies of God commented that it was this landmark event that prompted them to espouse a greater sense of urgency toward the matter of racial reconciliation in the church. On the day immediately following the Memphis Miracle, the Pentecostal Fellowship of North America was dissolved. In its wake, the Pentecostal and Charismatic Churches of North America (PCCNA) was formed by both white and Black denominations. Furthermore, in 1995, the General Council resolved to encourage the "inclusion of black brothers and sisters throughout every aspect of the Assemblies of God." To take this concern one step further, General Superintendent Thomas Trask appointed a committee to investigate the possibility of changing the General Presbytery and Executive Presbytery in order to reflect the Fellowship's demographic composition in a more genuine manner. Two years later, the General Council voted for the inclusion of representatives from ethnic fellowships within the General Presbytery as well as voting to expand the Executive Presbytery in order to include a representative from nonwhite racial/ethnic groups.

Another notable example of how the increasing influence of Pentecostalism as an ecclesial development within the Black Church tradition is the emergence of the Full Gospel Baptist Church Fellowship. In 1992, Bishop Paul S. Morton initiated a "spiritual gifts" movement with twelve fellow pastors from the National Baptist Convention, USA, Inc., an undertaking that eventually resulted in the formation of the Full Gospel Baptist Church Fellowship. The first Full Gospel Baptist Church Fellowship conference was held in New Orleans, Louisiana, in 1994, where the denominational headquarters remained until the devastation of Hurricane Katrina forced the Full Gospel Baptists to relocate to Atlanta, Georgia.

The Full Gospel Baptists represent a burgeoning set of denominations or voluntary organizations (primarily from an African American Baptist background) that accepts the operation of spiritual gifts (the *charismata*) within the church, which is in contrast to the doctrinal teachings of many Baptist congregations. Furthermore, whereas the Full Gospel Baptists are arguably based upon a *foundation* of Baptist doctrine, they embrace a wide range of charismatic influences akin to the Holiness and Pentecostal movements. Such influences include speaking in other tongues, prophecy, the baptism of the Holy Ghost, the "five-fold" ministry (apostles, prophets, pastors, teachers, and evangelists), and the acceptance of women in ministry in all ranks. There is a heavy emphasis on corporate praise and worship, and the denomination's governmental structure is based on an Episcopal hierarchy. Besides North America, the Full Gospel Baptist churches are rapidly expanding their membership and influence to Africa, Asia, the Caribbean, and Europe. In July 2013, Bishop Morton stepped down and announced that Bishop Joseph W. Walker III of Mt. Zion Baptist Church in Nashville, Tennessee, was named the denomination's new presiding bishop.

SEXISM AND THE "STAINED-GLASS CEILING" IN THE BLACK CHURCH TRADITION

A substantial challenge that continues to undermine Black Christianity's fullest expression as a liberating gospel as mandated in Galatians 3:27-28 is the ongoing institutional sexism and gender inequality within many of the denominations of the historic Black Church tradition. This is most clearly evident in the persistence of many Black churches to disavow Black women's call to the preaching ministry, deny their right to be ordained, and ultimately restrict any female ministers from providing pastoral leadership.

For example, in the nearly two centuries of the African Methodist Episcopal Church's existence, no woman had ever been appointed a bishop. But, in July 2000, Rev. Vashti Murphy McKenzie finally broke that barrier. With the solid support of her family, local church community, and the Delta Sigma Theta sorority, Reverend McKenzie was able to shatter what she called "the stained-glass ceiling" when she was named bishop of the 18th Episcopal District in Southeast Africa (composed of approximately two hundred churches and ten thousand members in Lesotho, Botswana, Swaziland, and Mozambique) of the AME Church. Her four-year appointment followed a successful ten-year stint as a pastor of Payne Memorial Church in Baltimore, Maryland, during which time she increased the membership from 300 to more than 1,700. Upon assuming her post, Bishop McKenzie declared, "One of the things we're looking to do is to respond to the numbers of children who are being abandoned [because] of AIDS." Toward that end, she pledged to concentrate on programs for grassroots economic development, construction of schools, and expanded health care delivery. Bishop McKenzie is one of a growing number of Black female preachers and pastors, including Rev. Dr. Renita Weems, Rev. Dr. Cynthia Hale, Rev. Dr. Cheryl J. Sanders, Rev. Dr. Claudette A. Copeland, Rev. Dr. Suzan Johnson Cook, Rev. Dr. Gina Stewart, and Rev. Dr. Teresa Fry Brown. These leaders refuse to allow either sexism or racism to hinder them from making a prophetic difference within the Black Church specifically and American society more generally.

THE RISE OF WOMANIST APPROACHES TO RELIGION AND THEOLOGY

In the late 1980s, the rise of womanist theology and ethics revolutionized the interpretation of African American religion with the recognition to include gender within the purview of liberation. The cause of providing a corrective—not only to the invisibility imposed upon race—is superseded only by the obfuscation of the centrality and value of Black women's presence and activity in the religious experience. The groundbreaking essay "Black Theology and Black Women" (1979) by systematic theologian Jacquelyn Grant offers a strong critique as well as a necessary corrective to the work of Black male theologians who promoted a narrow definition of liberation that utterly ignored the gender discrimination and misogyny suffered by Black women in a wholesale fashion. Grant's article served as a necessary spark that would eventually ignite the theological imagination and intellectual vitality that would later coalesce into the womanist movement.

Inspired by the term and concept of *womanist* as defined in novelist Alice Walker's text, *In Search of Our Mothers' Gardens* (1984), womanist theology offers intense and provocative critiques of the triple jeopardy of racism, sexism, and classism within both the Black Church and American society at large. In Walker's definition of "womanist" as both individual and movement, there are a number of guidelines that must be dealt with in order to understand womanism as a movement and ideology.[13] By arguing that ending sexual oppression must be as essential to liberation struggles as dismantling racial discrimination, womanist scholars such as Katie Cannon, Jacquelyn Grant, Delores Williams, Emilie Townes, Kelly Brown Douglas, and others were able to contend that the burden of the cross was best symbolized by the historic exploitation of Black women along lines of race, class, and gender.

Womanism finds its basis in notions inherent within African American theological and ethical perspectives such as a sense of community, a longing for justice, and a deep and personal love of oneself, of others, and of God. Taken as a whole, this definition of womanism involves an epistemology and vocation that are both challenging and affirmative. Offering the prospects for extensive research of Black women's activities within the Black Protestant tradition, Jualyne Dodson and Cheryl Townsend Gilkes contend that "if anything characterizes the role of black women in religion in America, it is the successful extension of their individual sense of regeneration, release, redemption and spiritual liberation to a collective ethos of struggle for and with the black community."[14]

121

In light of this situation, womanism as both a movement and an ideology serves as a model to other oppressed peoples to look internally, toward their own culture, institutions, and concerns, in order to improve their external conditions. In their constant quest for liberating knowledge, ethicist Emilie Townes asserts, "Womanists in the religious academy make great use of and have ongoing conversations with other academic disciplines."[15] In 2013, Rev. Dr. Emilie M. Townes became the dean and E. Rhodes and Leona B. Carpenter Professor of Womanist Ethics and Society of Vanderbilt Divinity School, the first African American woman to be dean of the school. Townes's ascendancy marks a significant sea change for womanist approaches to religion and theology as an interdisciplinary discourse and analysis in which it moves from the intellectual margins closer to the mainstream. In turn, the interpenetration of womanist insights into religious thought and praxis will hopefully provide the means for the edification and quickening of all oppressed peoples.

For example, the LGBTQ (lesbian, gay, bisexual, transgender, and queer) community, the elderly, the physically/mentally disadvantaged, and the poor are present in Alice Walker's vision of womanism, but it still remains to be seen if the actual embodiment of her vision will do the same within the auspices of the Black Church tradition and the broader African American community. As theologian Kelly Brown Douglas astutely illustrates, the desired goal of womanist approaches to religion and theology is that

> a·social-political analysis of wholeness will confront racism, sexism, classism, and heterosexism not only as they impinge upon the Black community, but also as they are nurtured within that community. It addresses the ways in which the Black community and Black institutions—that is, church, schools—perpetuate Black oppression. It does not seek to prioritize different forms of oppression, or to pit women against men/the poor against the rich. It does, however, seek to eliminate anything that prevent Black people from being whole, liberated people, and from living and working together as a whole, unified community. . . . But perhaps more importantly, a social-political analysis of wholeness challenges womanist scholars to forthrightly confront heterosexism within the Black church and community.[16]

Based on the sense of communal commitments and accountability that emerge from womanist ethics and theology, womanists will not allow the same kind of oversights that occurred in feminism such as those of heterosexism, ageism, or classism. Ethicist Katie Cannon asserts the core elements of a burgeoning womanist consciousness

> cannot be understood and explained adequately apart from the historical context in which Black women have found themselves as moral agents. By tracking down the central and formative facts in the Black woman's social world, one can identify the determinant and determining structures of oppression that have shaped the context in which Black women discriminately and critically interpret Scripture, in order to apprehend the divine Word from the perspective.[17]

Cannon's distinctive hermeneutical turn is indicated by her declaration that

> throughout the history of the United States, the interrelationship of White supremacy and Black patriarchal sexism has characterized Black women's reality as a situation of struggle—a struggle to survive in two contradictory worlds simultaneously, one White, privileged, and oppressive, the Black, exploited, and oppressed. Thus, an untangling of the Black religious heritage sheds light on the feminist consciousness that guides Black women in their ongoing struggle for survival.[18]

In describing a key transition from a Black male-dominated theology of liberation to womanist theological perspectives, theologian Delores Williams explains

> the difference between the female ethical effort and that of the black male liberation theologian is that the black female theologian, in her ethical task of revaluing, must also reconstruct and redeem from invisibility the life-world of African American women. On the basis of the reconstruction and redemption in this book an ethical principle emerges as a guide in identifying what is to be revalued. The ethical principle yielded is "survival and a positive quality of life for black women and their families in the presence and care of God."[19]

Nestled within the work of womanist scholars and their grasp of the complex interconnection of race, class, gender, and sexuality is a considerable wealth of insight about the growing edge of liberation. Addressing the primacy of Black women's religious experience, theologian Jacquelyn Grant asserts that

> womanist theology begins with the experiences of Black women as its point of departure. . . . These experiences provide a context which is significant for doing theology. Those experiences had been and continue to be defined by racism, sexism and classism and therefore offer a unique opportunity and a new challenge for developing a relevant perspective in the theological enterprise.[20]

Taken together, Black feminist thought and womanist theology have the potential to provide substantial inroads into how gender relations operate within the collective experiences of African Americans. Furthermore, moving forward, the reevaluation and reinterpretation of religious history that readily bespeaks a sacred tradition of Black women's sense and celebration of their relationship with the divine, their community, and themselves is a radical hermeneutical purview that intrinsically redefines the prospect of religious enterprise.[21]

THE BLACK CHURCH TRADITION
AND THE PRISON INDUSTRIAL COMPLEX

One of the greatest threats to the progressive social gains made in the United States is the mounting dramatic increase of incarceration of African Americans over the last thirty years. Even now, the prison-industrial complex in the United States is practically bursting at the seams, and it is largely comprised of Black folk who are the largest demographic in the current US prison population. Of the more than 2.1 million inmates imprisoned in the United States today, roughly one million are African American. Blacks make up 43.9 percent of the state and federal prison populations but only 12.3 percent of the US population. By contrast, whites account for 69 percent of the US population and 34.7 percent of those incarcerated.[22] In the 1930s, approximately 75 percent of prison admissions were white while 22 percent were African American. By 1992 those figures had been fundamentally reversed.[23]

One of every three Black men born today can expect to go to prison in his lifetime. At present, 1.4 million African American men (13 percent) have lost their right to vote as a result of a felony conviction—seven times the national average. Taking a more concentrated focus of this issue, in five states that deny ex-offenders the right to vote—Alabama, Florida, Iowa, Kentucky, and Virginia—one in four Black men is permanently disenfranchised.[24] There were 98,000 African Americans incarcerated in 1954 and 288,800 in 1984, as compared to the nearly one million either in prison or jail right now. While the Black prison population in the United States increased by 300 percent from 1954 to 1984, when calculated from 1954 to the present, the incarceration of Black women, men, and children has risen by a staggering 900 percent.[25]

Whereas Black men have too often been the focus of these imprisonment statistics, the fate of Black women has steadily become even more alarming and bespeaks the true crisis for every aspect of the Black community's survival. According to one report, between the years of 1980 and 1994, the number of women—primarily women of color—entering state and federal prisons rose by 386 percent.[26] Looking at that predicament in sharper focus, we are facing the reality that Black women born today are five times more likely to go to prison in their lifetime than Black women born in 1974. Put another way, one in every eighteen Black women born today can expect to go to jail in her lifetime; this is six times the rate of incarceration for white women. Finally, by the modest estimate, as of right now, on any given day, one of every fourteen Black children has a parent in prison.[27] In short, we can safely assume that, at this current rate, the continued growth of the prison system's impact on African Americans in years to come has the potential to lead to nothing less than the devastation of Black families, the decimation of Black communities, the systematic disenfranchisement of Black voters, and the destruction of any clear prospects for Black freedom and flourishing in the truest sense. Thus, if this expansion of the prison-industrial complex is not abated or even abolished soon, we could very well see in less than one lifetime a scenario wherein entire generations of Black families will be no longer be citizens, much less human beings, but rather state property under constant state supervision.

The deliberate criminalization of Black America served as a means of creating a smooth transformation of coerced Black labor from the plantation to prison. Although slavery was arguably abolished with passage of the Thirteenth Amendment of the Constitution in 1865, there is more here than meets the eye. The text of the amendment reads as follows: "Neither slavery nor involuntary servitude, *except as a punishment for crime whereof the party shall have been duly convicted*, shall exist within the United States, or any place subject to their jurisdiction"[28] (emphasis added). Two problems surface from that legislation. First, since the word *slavery* is not mentioned in the Constitution until the Thirteenth Amendment, it could be argued that the document that ended chattel slavery effectively inserted it into the law of the land. Second, by stipulating slavery as a punishment for crime, the Thirteenth Amendment essentially conflates slavery with criminality in ways that could be twisted to the clear disadvantage of the newly freed Black populace and their children.

In the years after the Civil War, a series of laws known as the Black Codes sprang up throughout the US South. The Black Codes were established by white lawmakers in the former Confederate states, with the specific goal of declaring vague actions—such as "vagrancy," "mischief," "disturbing the peace," and making "insulting gestures"—as crimes if committed by "free Negroes." Very often, the Black Codes went into effect when free Blacks were not working on behalf of their former slaveholding elites or had the audacity to behave as if they were actually free. Moreover, many Black Southerners were likely to be rounded up for cheap labor on chain gangs or in prison sweatshops in Alabama, Mississippi, Louisiana, Georgia, the Carolinas, and Tennessee by local authorities who collected fees from former slave owners and private contractors who could literally work the free Black population to death because, as "criminals," they had few rights and virtually no legal recourse. Even worse, the *de facto* criminalization of Black people since the Civil War also has had the perverse effect in the broad scope of American public opinion of creating the impression that they deserve whatever fate befalls them because being a criminal means they are neither a citizen nor a creature made by God.

More than a century ago, W. E. B. DuBois—that majestic scholar of the African American experience—discussed this dilemma of criminalization in his seminal work, *The Souls of Black Folk.* By discussing the early phase of the prison-industrial complex in action, DuBois recognizes that

> daily the Negro is coming more and more to look upon law and justice, not as protecting safeguards, but as sources of humiliation and oppression. The laws are made by men who have little interest in him; they are executed by men who have absolutely no motive for treating the black people with courtesy or consideration; and, finally, the accused law-breaker is tried, not by his peers, but too often by men who would rather punish ten innocent Negroes than let one guilty one escape.[29]

But, before going any further, readers ought not to think that this creates an argument stating that a Black person should never be found guilty and punished for a crime he or she committed, because that is certainly not the case. To the contrary, the overarching concern is the fact that the legal system is so fundamentally flawed that the historic stigma of criminality has become virtually inescapable; anyone who doubts this simply has to reflect on the premise of racial profiling and other modes of institutional racism within the American criminal justice system. Without a doubt, a bleak situation that was once a distasteful possibility from DuBois's perspective a century ago is now becoming a disastrous reality.

More recently, legal scholar Michelle Alexander argues rigorously and persuasively that, despite the presumption of racial progress and interracial harmony embodied in the political victories of Barack Obama and the triumphant dominance of Oprah Winfrey, Shawn "Jay-Z" Carter, and Beyoncé Knowles in both the financial and cultural realms, the preponderance of racism in American society has not ended, but it has merely been redesigned in an unrelenting fashion. In recent decades, the mass incarceration of African Americans has become a formidable system of social control based on race, class, gender, and institutionalized oppression within the nation's criminal justice system. Alexander reviews the dynamics of racial inequality and the law through the prism of American racial history from the colonial era to the present and effectively delineates the institutionalization of racial segregation and racist stereotypes prevalent in the Jim and Jane Crow era serving as justification for the so-called "war on drugs" of the 1980s and 1990s. She offers a keen analysis of how mass incarceration has had an increasingly devastating effect upon African Americans who, as former inmates, will be legally discriminated against for the rest of their lives by being denied employment, housing, education, and numerous public benefits.[30]

The grave concern in this regard is what happens when the nation's privately owned prison system, rather than the Black family, church, or school, serves as the most prevalent institution and definitive source of Black racial identification for today's youth. In light of this situation, churches must work with due haste to realign such thinking within ourselves as well as within the younger generations that are now coming of age.

Incorporated on September 17, 2003, the Samuel DeWitt Proctor Conference (SDPC) Inc. is a network of several thousand progressive Black pastors, scholars, activists, and lay leaders drawn from varying denominational backgrounds who have taken on the crisis of mass incarceration threatening the African American community. In keeping with the visionary life and legacy of the late Rev. Dr. Samuel DeWitt Proctor, the SDPC's core founders—Dr. Iva E. Carruthers, Rev. Dr. Frederick D. Haynes III, and Rev. Dr. Jeremiah A. Wright Jr.—met, prayed, talked, and envisioned together about a particular entity that could speak to those who have a deep hunger for making Black prophetic witness committed to social justice and public advocacy rooted in sound biblical knowledge and Black liberation theology. From its genesis, the SDPC always affirmed in its organizational ethos that there should be no separation between divine justice and social justice that the Holy Spirit calls all Christians to engage in on a daily basis in the communities and congregations that they inhabit. The SDPC was originally established with the hope and faith that the organization's key activities proclaimed in the biblical mandate of Luke 4:18-19: "to proclaim release to the captives and recovery of sight to the blind, to let the oppressed go free" (NRSV). As such, SDPC has entered into the public square in numerous campaigns as a divine calling with the intention of challenging the hearts, minds, and souls of clergy, laity, activists, seminarians, and intellectuals from communities and churches nationwide, with prayerful dedication and divinely inspired purpose toward changing the sociopolitical landscape for the next generation of those working for social justice. Since the late 2000s, this organization has emphasized the dismantling of mass incarceration by confronting both the causes and consequences of the failed "war on drugs" and the endemic structural inequalities associated with it by raising public awareness and promoting direct action to reform the criminal justice system.

BLACK MEGACHURCHES AND THE "PROSPERITY GOSPEL"

One of the most profound transformations in the past forty years of the Black Church tradition has been the emergence of megachurches. The term *megachurch* essentially refers to any congregation with a sustained average attendance of several thousand people in its weekly worship services as well as the church's overall membership. Whereas most discussions of megachurches focus on very large white evangelical congregations—there are currently more than 1,200 such fellowships in the United States—there is a growing proliferation of African American megachurches gaining the national spotlight.

While size is the most immediately apparent characteristic of these congregations, the Black megachurches in the United States generally share many other traits. "Megachurches," ethicist Jonathan Walton writes,

> are characterized by colossal edifices that house not only sanctuaries that seat thousands of people but [also] child care centers, gymnasiums, bookstores, and a host of other business ventures. . . . In major metropolitan areas . . . megachurches have become both standard-bearer and a staple of African American religious life. As a result, megachurch pastors have become spiritual icons and national celebrities within the black community.[31]

Although often treated as a recent phenomenon within the Black Christian experience, there are actually examples of prominent Black megachurch pastors drawn from the twentieth century including Rev. Adam Clayton Powell Sr., Rev. Adam Clayton Powell Jr., Rev. J. M. Gates, Rev. C. L. Franklin, Prophet Jim ("Messiah in Mink") Jones, Elder Solomon Lightfoot Michaux, and Rev. Frederick J. ("Rev. Ike") Eikerenkoetter, to name only a few of the most celebrated ones. Some of the more renowned contemporary Black megachurches of this sort include Rev. Dr. Frederick K. C. Price's Crenshaw Christian Center; Bishop T. D. Jakes's The Potter's House; Rev. Tony Evans's Oak Cliff Bible Fellowship, all in Dallas, Texas; Bishop Joseph W. Walker III's Mt. Zion Full Gospel Baptist Church in Nashville, Tennessee; Rev. Kirbyjon Caldwell's Windsor Village United Methodist Church in Houston, Texas; Bishop Eddie Long's New Birth Missionary Baptist Church; and Rev. Creflo Dollar's World Changers Church in Atlanta, Georgia.

Despite the seeming abundance of prosperity-minded conservative megachurch pastors, there are also several examples of thriving Black megachurches that espouse a liberal or progressive theology committed to social justice such as Rev. Floyd H. Flake's Greater Allen AME Cathedral in Jamaica, New York, in Queens; Rev. Otis Moss III's Trinity United Church of Christ in Chicago, Illinois; Rev. Calvin O. Butts's Abyssinian Baptist Church in Harlem, New York; Rev. Dr. Gary Simpson's Concord Baptist Church in Brooklyn, New York; Rev. J. Alfred Smith's Allen AME Church in Oakland, California; Rev. Cecil Williams's Glide United Methodist Church in San Francisco, California; and Rev. Dr. Frederick D. Haynes III's Friendship West Baptist Church in Dallas, Texas, to name a few.

In his seminal work on African American religious institutions, W. E. B. DuBois observed that the Black church's key role in the local community was to provide a total support system for its members.[32] In this spirit, Black megachurches host a whole multitude of social, recreational, and aid ministries for their congregations. Likewise, most megachurches employ intentional efforts at enhancing congregational community, such as home fellowships and "cell churches" qua interest-based small-group meetings. These megachurches also illustrate the suburbanization of African American Christianity, especially in the rapidly growing urban areas in the southern Sun Belt of the United

States. These large churches often tend to occupy prominent tracts of land with tens of acres near major traffic thoroughfares. Most typically, Black megachurches tend to grow to their great size within a very short period of time, usually in less than ten years, and under the tenure of a single senior pastor. Contrary to expectations, these congregations promote intense personal commitment and loyalty in a majority of their members but also contain a large percentage of casual and anonymous spectators in their ranks due to the multimedia ministries (book publications, internet, television, and radio) that are often used as a form of evangelistic outreach. Although the senior pastors of these megachurches often have an authoritative style of preaching and church administration, typically they have extensive support teams of associate ministers and often retain hundreds of employees as full-time staff.

Since the new megachurch movement is still a fairly recent phenomenon, it is unclear in a historical sense how the size, demographics, and longevity of these congregations would extend beyond the tenure of their current and/or founding pastors. Evidence suggests, however, that these churches might remain vital following a shift in leadership from the founder to his successor as long as they service what theologian Paul Tillich says is the notion of religion as "ultimate concern" for their gathered worshipers.[33] But, as theologian Anthony B. Pinn notes:

> even black churches that have no interest in the megachurch phenomenon are likely to find themselves forced to respond. It is possible that these megachurches, particularly the nondenominational ones, will challenge the vitality of more traditionally aligned denominational churches because of their doctrinal and structural flexibility. Whether an active participant or not, black churches in the twenty-first century will have no choice but to think about their ministries and audience in terms of the megachurch phenomenon and its interpretation of the gospel.[34]

A majority of these megachurches have a conservative evangelical theology with a strong tendency of preaching a so-called prosperity gospel, which is basically defined as "the belief that material wealth is God's desire for the faithful."[35] In order to fully understand the Black Church tradition in its historic as well as contemporary forms, it is important to recognize the ways in which both the church and the broader African American community have been held captive to the ravages of capitalism. Although African Americans perennially have been on a shaky economic foundation, every leading statistical indicator—wages and income, unemployment rates, accumulated wealth, educational attainment, bankruptcy, and liquid assets—reveals that the Black populace in the United States is currently facing an economic situation that is crumbling at a faster, more devastating rate than virtually every demographic sector in the US population.[36]

Since its inception, the scholarly study of the Black Church in North America has been concerned with the material as well as the spiritual realities of the African American community. For instance, in his inaugural study of the Black religious experience, historian W. E. B. DuBois asserted that the Black Church has had a complex mission tied to providing the means for human flourishing for the African American community in a myriad of ways.[37] In recognition of its existence as a prime locus for the struggle for freedom, justice, and equality, critical examinations of the Black Church have been focused on its perennial commitment to linking the idealistic promises of divine justice with the material prospects of social justice here on earth. When assessing the traditional functionality of the Black Church, historian Manning Marable notes that this venerable institution "became the way out, the forum in which each week's mountain of frustrations and tragedies are eliminated from one's consciousness, a holy place of peace in a world of utter madness and dark decay."[38] As the Black community made its historic transition from slavery to freedom, Black churches strove to fulfill the deepest yearnings of Black men, women, and children in terms of both their physical realities as well as their spiritual concerns. Put another way, in order to understand the sacred and secular experiences of African Americans in their totality, attention must be paid to the immaterial and material dimensions of Black life.

Much like the megachurch, it is important to place the prevailing concerns about the "prosperity gospel" in historical perspective. Given the Black Church's vital role as a "refuge" and "surrogate world," however, there was a troubling chasm between the conservative and prophetic dimensions of Black Christian thought and praxis that developed during the twentieth century.[39] During the 1930s, Benjamin E. Mays and Joseph W. Nicholson conducted research on the Black Church, wherein they randomly analyzed the content of one hundred sermons by Black preachers. Their data found that fifty-four sermons were generally "pie-in-the sky," otherworldly sensibility in nature, while twenty sermons reflected identifiable theological doctrines, and the remaining twenty-six focused on contemporary social issues, thus suggesting a widening chasm between the Black clergy and the oppressed majority of the nation's Black populace.[40]

At the height of the civil rights movement, the sociologist E. Franklin Frazier observed, "The Negro Church has lost much of its influence as an agency of social control. Its supervision over the marital and family life of Negroes has declined. The church has ceased to be the chief means of economic cooperation."[41] Although written many decades ago, Frazier's commentary could just as easily apply to the contemporary state of the Black Church tradition. Even now, an interesting paradox has taken place in matters of Black faith and culture wherein there is a declining significance of the historic Black Church denominations on the one hand and a startling level of growth amongst churches espousing prosperity gospel theology on the other hand. In this instance, making sense of patterns of growth and decline within various expressions of Black Christianity resides in examining discourses and dynamics of class as representing Paul Tillich's notion of "ultimate concern."[42]

THE BLACK CHURCH TRADITION AND THE QUEST FOR ECONOMIC JUSTICE

The move toward a concerted study of the interplay of religion and economic forces is a vital and fruitful move for Black Church studies to make, not least because of the continuing levels of discrimination, disadvantage, and death faced by African Americans in the context of our current economic recession. In a sermon at the National Cathedral in Washington, DC, on March 31, 1968, Rev. Dr. Martin Luther King Jr. articulated two key truths about the contemporary context in which we live. First, contrary to the conventional wisdom about modern economic theory throughout the twentieth century, Dr. King, as the nation's foremost civil rights leader, asserted that the majority of hardships that humans endure such as transgenerational poverty, homelessness, unemployment, chronic illness, infant mortality, lackluster education, and imprisonment could be remedied by the affluence of American society if the people acknowledged that the nation had the capability and capacity to end structural inequality and spiritual misery both at home and abroad. Second and more important, Dr. King boldly asserted more than four decades ago that, regardless of how dreadful things might seem, impoverishment and scarcity of resources are human rather than divine creations. In other words, in a global context wherein practically anything can be grown, manufactured, or repaired on demand, poverty is much more about an inequitable distribution of the world's resources due to wanton greed and reckless indifference of mortal beings instead of being some curse by a distant and indifferent God.

Presently, Black Church history must contend with the dual concerns of economic justice and globalization in a more direct, thoughtful, and straightforward manner. In countless seminary classrooms and university lecture halls, we have a steady and valid condemnation of prosperity gospel, faith-based initiatives, compassionate conservatism, and the rising popularity of megachurches that perpetuate a "Christianity Lite" version of the gospel that is seen as a threat that pervades too much of the contemporary theological and ecclesial energies within the Black community. Conversely, however, there is a frightening scarcity of alternative notions of how to confront this "name it and claim it" spirituality in a truly formidable way.[43] In essence, those of us committed to Black Church studies have spoken about what we *are against* but have not said what we *stand for*.

Simply stated, when stripped of any ideological or philosophical jargon, economic justice refers to the understanding of *who* gets *what, when, where,* and *how.* As this point in history illustrates, African American church leaders and congregations of the historic Black Church tradition have the greatest need for this knowledge yet are often ill equipped to discuss what is at stake for Black people in an era that is being overwhelmingly defined by the rampant consolidation of wealth and power in the midst of relentless misery and depravation. Moreover, even as Black Church studies programs should position themselves to articulate the who, what, when, where, and how regarding the ways in which the political economy works, only concerted efforts within theological education would provide the means by which we could cultivate ethical leadership that would have the moral resolve to ask why the unjust exploitation of natural resources, the amalgamation of corporate power, and the unfettered amassing of wealth worldwide has surpassed sound stewardship and fair distribution of the planet's plentiful blessings, both human and otherwise, and serve as a basis for renewed moral vision and social action.

BLACK CHURCHES AND PRESIDENTIAL POLITICS IN THE POST–CIVIL RIGHTS ERA

Throughout US history, the majority of Black political leadership in the United States has been fomented within the Black Church tradition. Since Christian ministry was the most prevalent and respectable profession available to African Americans—most particularly to men—and churches were the only corporate institutions under the sole control of Blacks, the training and development of Black clergy often coincided with the cultivation of Black leadership. As such, Black political leadership dating back to the Reconstruction era can trace its origins back to the church with many of these figures having been ministers as well. Conversely, as W. E. B. DuBois, Carter G. Woodson, and other scholars of the Black Church tradition have noted, the Black preacher was typically the most highly educated member of the Black community and ultimately served as a mediator between the oppressed Black populace and the mainstream society. Thanks in large part to the political, social, and cultural gains resulting from the civil rights movement, increasing numbers of Black women and men have joined the ranks of the educated and professional middle class.

Largely inspired by the ethos of the Black Church tradition, the civil rights movement in the United States helped expand and ostensibly

135

redefine the democratic possibilities of American society. For example, the Southern Christian Leadership Conference (SCLC) was formed in January 1957 with Rev. Dr. Martin Luther King Jr. as one of its founders. By mobilizing thousands of activists and protesters to stage massive campaigns of nonviolent civil disobedience across the American South, the SCLC proved itself to be one of the most definitive and effective civil rights organizations throughout the 1960s and 1970s. Many of the signature events in the popular memory of the civil rights movement—the "Battle of Birmingham," the 1963 March on Washington for Jobs and Freedom, and the 1965 "Bloody Sunday" protest march from Selma to Montgomery, Alabama, among others—were calculated tactical efforts coordinated in part by the SCLC to push the US federal government to dismantle segregation, namely through the passage of the Civil Rights Act of 1964 and the Voting Rights Act of 1965. With King's able leadership of the SCLC in its heyday, the undertaking was most noteworthy for revealing the ability of Black clergy and laity to use moral suasion in order to advance the goals of the civil rights movement amongst supporters not only across racial and ethnic lines but also across the gamut of faith traditions ranging from Protestantism, Catholicism, Judaism, Islam, and Hinduism to even humanism and atheism.

The political mobilization of Black churches has been a major issue that has caused much consternation amongst the growing ranks of American conservatism, especially the Religious Right, over the past four decades. A key example of this issue is evident in Rev. Jesse Jackson's national campaigns for the Democratic Party's nomination for the US presidency in 1984 and 1988. In fact, Jackson's presidential bid was highly indicative of a long-standing paradigm of leadership within Black America that merged religion and politics. As a Black preacher with a proven pedigree of prophetic ministry and political activism, Jackson's candidacy for the Democratic nomination was able to mobilize Black churches nationwide to organize voter registration drives and political rallies. In this fashion, Reverend Jackson followed in the distinctive footsteps of Dr. King as well as Rev. Adam Clayton Powell Jr., the renowned senior pastor of Abyssinian Baptist Church (1938–71) who served fourteen terms in the House of Representatives for his Harlem congressional district, by bringing the spiritual and political aspirations of African Americans and white progressives into closer alignment than ever before. Especially with the 1988 campaign, Jackson became the embodiment of the desires for greater inclusion and enfranchisement not only by the Black community and other people of color but also by the poor and disadvantaged groups. The successful groundswell amongst a voting community that was previously alienated and apathetic soon became sparked by Jackson's political campaigns and illustrated his effectiveness in galvanizing this level of support from the body politic.

Although Jackson's presidential aspirations were never fulfilled, he and millions of his supporters across the United States strove to renew the spirit of the civil rights movement by advancing the Black Church tradition's mission of social justice as the benchmark of a more hopeful, inclusive political vision for America in the post–civil rights era. In both presidential races, Jackson ran on what many considered to be a very liberal political platform, also declaring that he wanted to create a "Rainbow Coalition" of various marginalized groups, including African Americans, Latino/as, the working poor, women, members of the LGBTQ (lesbian, gay, bisexual, transgender, and queer) community, and progressive whites who did not fit into any of the aforementioned categories.

However, a major controversy erupted during the early stages of the 1984 campaign when Jackson reportedly made disparaging remarks, referring to Jews as "hymies" and to New York City as "Hymietown"; amidst the uproar over these slurs, he later issued an apology for remarks and was still able to run successful nationwide campaigns.[44] Jackson, who had been written off by pundits as a fringe candidate with little chance at winning the nomination, surprised many when he took third place behind Senator Gary Hart and former Vice President Walter Mondale, who eventually won the nomination. Jackson garnered 3.5 million votes and won five primaries, all in the South. Four years later, his past accomplishments made him seem to be a more credible candidate for the Democratic nomination in 1988, especially since he was both better financed and better organized. Consequently, Jackson once again exceeded expectations as he more than doubled his previous results, capturing 6.9 million votes and winning eleven primaries.

More than simply lending moral support and ministerial endorsements, Black churches were instrumental to Jackson's political successes because they were mobilized and directly involved in the local organization of his statewide campaigns, sponsoring rallies, enlisting volunteers, holding voter registration drives, and transporting voters to the polls. In many respects, Jackson's presidential runs, in addition to the influential political careers of Rev. William H. Gray III, Rev. Walter E. Fauntroy, Rev. Andrew Young, and Rev. Floyd H. Flake, among others, have been seen as a logical continuation of the political goals of the civil rights movement.[45]

With his landmark election as the forty-fourth president of the United States, Barack H. Obama Jr. has ignited a veritable cottage industry within the world of publishing with a flood of biographies, social and cultural analyses, and histories about modern democracy, civil rights, and postwar American race relations. The best of these books have attempted to examine America's tortured history of race relations through the prism of Mr. Obama's unique biography and unparalleled political ambitions.[46] With its lyrical meditations on race, identity, and consciousness, Obama's memoir, *Dreams from My Father* (1995), helped create a portrait of the young future president as a perpetual cultural outsider who was forced to deal with issues of belonging in a world marked by racial stratification. For instance, historian James T. Kloppenberg places Obama in the wider context of the American political tradition and chronicles Obama's development in the framework of the history of American democracy in the ideas of "philosophical pragmatism, and the intellectual turmoil of the 1980s and 1990s" in an effort to understand the president's vision of American politics and culture.[47]

Even though it is an ambitious and worthwhile goal to identify President Obama as both a genuine intellectual and a serious student of American pragmatism tracing both intellectual pedagogical experiences that shape Obama's schooling and the historical context that impacted his time at Punahou Academy, Occidental College, Columbia University, and Harvard University Law School, it can just as easily be argued that the two decades he spent worshiping at the Trinity United Church of Christ were equally as influential in shaping his political and moral compass. During the 1980s and 1990s, Obama's intellectual evolution rested on intense study as well as practical experience as first, a community organizer in the South Side of Chicago and later, a University of Chicago law professor and Illinois state senator. The sum of his experiences made him a keen student of American history in addition to being deeply appreciative of the contours of American democracy as a fluid ongoing conversation rather than a fixed predetermined destination. Kloppenberg observes that Mr. Obama's "predilection to conciliate whenever possible is grounded in his understanding of the history of American thought culture and politics," yet critics would argue that Mr. Obama's sophisticated understanding of history and politics has been overwhelmed by the harsh realities of governance in an era of hyperpartisan national politics.[48] In terms of both his biological and biographical background, President Obama literally embodies a somewhat conflicted albeit resilient identity. And yet it is precisely this complexity, with all of its intrinsic tensions, complicated contradictions, and ambiguous anxieties, that might ironically serve as the common ground shared by an increasing majority of Americans.

As a story of Obama's religious journey, *Dreams from My Father* serves as testament of faith. To be biracial, to have belonged to a non-religious home and a Christian church, to have attended a largely Muslim school in Indonesia, ultimately to have embraced the Black liberation theology espoused by Trinity United Church of Christ (UCC) in urban Chicago, to be more than one thing and sometimes not fully anything—this is an increasingly common experience for Americans, including many racial/ethnic minorities. Mr. Obama has spoken often and eloquently about the importance of religion in public life. But, like many political leaders wary of offending potential backers in a society rooted in First Amendment rights, he has been less revealing about what he believes—about God, about prayer, and about the connection between personal salvation and moral responsibility. In some respects, his reluctance is understandable in light of America's ongoing "culture wars." Mr. Obama's religiosity has been portrayed as unconventional and politically problematic based on a traditional political paradigm but might actually speak more honestly to the notions of lived faith at the dawn of the twenty-first century. By his own account, Mr. Obama was born on the one hand to a white American mother who was a Christian-turned-secular humanist and on the other hand to a native African father who was a Muslim-turned-atheist. Furthermore, it is because of an early childhood traveling and living all across the world with plenty of spiritual influences but without any particular religion that Obama's faith developed the way it did.

Therefore, when he made the journey to become an avowed Christian in the early 1990s, having been baptized at Trinity UCC in Chicago by Rev. Dr. Jeremiah A. Wright Jr., Obama actually portrays a more contemporary vision of Black religious faith formation. As Obama describes his earliest meeting with Wright in *Dreams from My Father*, "It became clear in that very first meeting that, despite the reverend's frequent disclaimers, it was this capacious talent of his—this ability to hold together, if not reconcile, the conflicting strains of the black experience—upon which Trinity's success had ultimately been built."[49] Yet, in a bitter twist of fate, it would be Mr. Obama's commitment to the Black Church tradition that became a potentially devastating flashpoint of the 2008 presidential campaign. In March 2008, a media firestorm erupted when video excerpts of Dr. Wright's sermons were taken out of context and picked up by worldwide media outlets. Republican rivals and conservative pundits frequently used Dr. Wright's words in order to question the patriotism of Mr. Obama, at that time a front-running Democratic presidential candidate. Since Mr. Obama and his family were members of Trinity UCC, the media scrutiny over Obama and Wright's relationship made Trinity a focal point of the ensuing controversy that unfolded from Dr. Wright's first appearances in his own defense in the mainstream media to Obama's public resignation from Trinity Church.

Dr. Wright will be linked forever to the political turmoil that arose during the historic 2008 presidential campaign of the then senator Barack Obama. Although Wright was unwillingly thrust into the spotlight, the media attention could neither overshadow his prophetic teachings nor define his life and ministry. As a legendary faith leader and human rights activist in Chicago's South Side community, Rev. Dr. Jeremiah A. Wright Jr. has worked tirelessly for over forty years to unite social justice and divine justice for poor and marginalized peoples both here and worldwide. A lifelong proponent of higher education as a means of personal and communal empowerment, Wright has four earned degrees, a Bachelor of Arts and Master of Arts in English from Howard University, a Master of Arts in the History of Religions from the University of Chicago Divinity School, and a Doctor of Ministry from the United Theological Seminary under the tutelage of Rev. Dr. Samuel DeWitt Proctor. Trained as a historian of religions as well as a student of Black Sacred Music, ethnomusicology, and African diasporan studies, he helped Christians nationwide make the connection among their spiritual faith, African history, and cultural heritage. In addition, he is also the author of numerous scholarly articles for academic journals as well as the author of numerous texts that are widely used in seminaries and theological institutions across the globe: *What Makes You So Strong?*; *Good News!: Sermons of Hope for Today's Families*; *Africans Who Shaped Our Faith*; *When Black Men Stand Up for God*; *Blow the Trumpet in Zion!: Global Vision and Action for the 21st Century Black Church*; and most recently, *A Sankofa Moment: The History of Trinity United Church of Christ*.

Moreover, as senior pastor emeritus of Trinity UCC in Chicago, Illinois, where he served faithfully for thirty-six years, Wright combined his studies of African traditional religions, African/African American musicology, and the historic Black Church tradition with his academic studies of Judeo-Christian thought to develop some fifty pioneering ministries such as HIV/AIDS outreach programs, two senior housing complexes, a federally funded child-care program for low-income families, and TUCC's Kwame Nkrumah Academy. Dr. Wright has inspired not only his congregation but also an entire nation to imagine a more progressive and prophetic example of church leadership by moving ministry, as he often proclaims, "from theory to praxis." Since 2003 Dr. Wright also has been a cofounder and board member of the Samuel DeWitt Proctor Conference, a national network that serves thousands of pastors, lay leaders, and community activists in addition to preparing the next generation of those working for social justice. In this fashion, Dr. Wright continues to serve as a mentor and role model for an entire generation of clergy, activists, and scholars seeking that which addresses the needs of the community as well as enriching the faith-filled lives and guaranteeing the human dignity of all people. Even as the media firestorm surrounding his controversial sound bite became ratings fodder for conservative politicos and right-wing media pundits, this long and esteemed career in ministry has been grossly obscured from popular memory as a whole. Nonetheless, the relevance of his ministry reaches far beyond his pastorate at Trinity UCC; Dr. Wright's ministry has transcended to a global stage with a liberating message of freedom, justice, and equality.[50] Rather than coming to the matter of faith bound by preexisting issues of traditionalism or preordained notions of Black racial identity to dictate his decision to affiliate himself with any given church, President Obama's relationship to the Black Church tradition under the spiritual guidance of Dr. Wright was the result of clear choice instead of being the result of coercion, chance, or circumstance. Researchers for years to come will have to contemplate and consider the significance of the nation's first Black president being under the tutelage and spiritual guidance of a pastor who was a proud and prophetic exemplar of Black liberation theology both in theory and praxis.

CONCLUSION

The experience of Black Christians in America resists any single interpretation or monolithic definition. Demonstrated by the various phases of development of African American Christendom from the Middle Passage to today's megachurches, the historic Black Church tradition continues to be shaped by the personal as well as collective experiences of African peoples who maintained spiritual faith in the midst of enslavement and emancipation alike. Facing the challenges of a new millennium, many Black Christians have inherited an enduring faith that saw their ancestors overcome the brutal dehumanization of chattel slavery, the tragic domination of Jim and Jane Crow segregation, and countless other nameless, unimaginable horrors. Discussing the history of Black Christianity in today's society means confronting a host of complicated issues yet realizing that the foundation of this faith remains intact: the belief that Black people are divinely created and represent God's plan for the world.

NOTES

INTRODUCTION: LESSONS THE DARK PAST HAS TAUGHT ME

1. Cornel West, *Race Matters* (Boston: Beacon Press, 1993), 14–15.

2. James H. Cone, *God of the Oppressed*, rev. ed. (1975; Maryknoll, NY: Orbis, 1997), xiii.

3. Vincent G. Harding, *Hope and History: Why We Must Share the Story of the Movement* (Maryknoll, NY: Orbis, 1997), 10.

4. James A. Baldwin, *The Fire Next Time* (1963; New York: Vintage, 1991), 47.

5. Cone, *God of the Oppressed*, xi.

6. C. Eric Lincoln and Lawrence Mamiya, *The Black Church in the African American Experience* (Durham, NC: Duke University Press, 1990), 3–4.

7. The phrase "kingdom and kin-dom of God" is somewhat of a compromise between two theological outlooks about the perceived human-Divine relationship. On the one hand, "kingdom of God" refers to the absolute sovereignty of God over all of creation as the "King of kings and Lord of lords." On the other hand, the "kin-dom of God" envisions humanity as being brought together as one family (hence the notion of "kin"), brought into unity with the Divine through Jesus Christ as God incarnate. Whereas many traditional Christians are familiar and typically more comfortable with the former phrase, it has overtones that are evocative of imperial might and gendered domination that a growing number of people find rather unsettling. Conversely, talking about being part of the family of God via "kin-dom" offers a more inclusive, loving, humane, and compassionate alternative vision of God's connection to human beings as part of creation that allows folks to reconsider contemporary Christian principles and practices from the viewpoint emphasizing God's love rather than God's power.

8. Saint Augustine, *The Confessions of Saint Augustine*, trans. Edward Bouverie Pusey, bk. 10, accessed December 20, 2013, http://www.sacred-texts.com/chr/augconf/aug10.htm.

9. James Loewen, *Lies My Teacher Told Me: Everything Your American History Textbook Got Wrong*, rev. ed. (New York: Touchstone, 2007).

10. Robin W. Winks, *The Historian as Detective: Essays on Evidence* (New York: Harper & Row, 1969).

11. George Santayana, *The Life of Reason or The Phases of Human Progress*, vol. 1, *Reason in Common Sense* (1905; New York: Scribners, 1917).

12. Robert Warrior, "Canaanites and Conquerors: Deliverance, Conquest, and Liberation Theology Today," *Christianity and Crisis* 49, no. 12 (September 11, 1989): 261–65; Itumeleng J. Mosala, *Biblical Hermeneutics and Black Theology in South Africa* (Grand Rapids, MI: Eerdmans, 1989); Cone, *God of the Oppressed*, xii; Vincent G. Harding, "The Uses of the Afro-American Past," in *The Religious Situation*, 1969, ed. Donald R. Cutter (Boston: Beacon, 1969), 829–40; Albert J. Raboteau, "African Americans, Exodus, and the American Israel" in *African-American Christianity*, ed. Paul E. Johnson (Berkeley: University of California Press, 1994), 1–17; Eddie S. Glaude Jr., *Exodus!: Religion, Race, and Nation in Early Nineteenth-Century Black America* (Chicago: University of Chicago Press, 2000), 143–67.

13. See Cain Hope Felder, ed., *Stony the Road We Trod: African American Biblical Interpretation* (Minneapolis: Fortress Press, 1991).

14. T. S. Eliot, *The Waste Land and Other Poems*, ed. Helen Vendler (1922; New York: Signet Classic, 1998), 21.

1. WAKING THE NATIONS UNDERGROUND

1. John Lovell Jr., *Black Song: The Forge and the Flame; The Story of How the Afro-American Spiritual Was Hammered Out* (New York: Paragon House, 1972), 368.

2. W. E. B. DuBois, *The Souls of Black Folk*, ed. David W. Blight and Robert Gooding-Williams (1903; Boston: Bedford/St. Martin's Press, 1997), 187.

3. Charles H. Long, "Passage and Prayer: The Origin of Religion in the Atlantic World," in *The Courage to Hope: From Black Suffering to Human Redemption*, ed. Quinton H. Dixie and Cornel West (Boston: Beacon Press, 1999).

4. Melville J. Herskovits, *The Myth of the Negro Past* (New York: Harper & Brothers, 1941); John W. Blassingame, *The Slave Community: Plantation Life in the Antebellum South* (New York: Oxford University Press, 1972); Henry Mitchell, *Black Belief: Folk Beliefs of Blacks in America and West Africa* (New York: Harper & Row, 1975); Orlando Patterson, *Slavery and Social Death: A Comparative Study* (Cambridge, MA: Harvard University Press, 1982); Peter Kolchin, *American Slavery: 1619–1877* (New York: Hill and Wang, 1993); Joseph E. Holloway, ed., *Africanisms in American Culture* (Bloomington: Indiana University Press, 1990); Michael A. Gomez, *Exchanging*

Our Country Marks: The Transformation of African Identities in the Colonial and Antebellum South (Chapel Hill: University of North Carolina Press, 1998); David Brion Davis, *In the Image of God: Religion, Moral Values, and Our Heritage of Slavery* (New Haven, CT: Yale University Press, 2001).

5. Vincent G. Harding, "Black Power and the American Christ," in *Black Theology: A Documentary History*, vol. 1, 1966–1979, ed. Gayraud S. Wilmore and James H. Cone (Maryknoll, NY: Orbis, 1979), 36.

6. Albert J. Raboteau, *Slave Religion: The "Invisible Institution" in the Antebellum South* (New York: Oxford University Press, 1978), chap. 2.

7. Mechal Sobel, *The World They Made Together: Black and White Values in Eighteenth-Century Virginia* (Princeton, NJ: Princeton University Press, 1987); Margaret Washington Creel, *A Peculiar People: Slave Religion and Community Culture among the Gullahs* (New York: New York University Press, 1988); Peter H. Wood, *Black Majority: Negroes in Colonial South Carolina from 1670 through the Stono Rebellion* (1974; New York: Norton, 1996).

8. For a broad, baseline discussion of a shared Central and West African religious heritage that was taken and transplanted in the Americas as a result of the Transatlantic Slave Trade, see Herskovits, *The Myth of the Negro Past*; Mechal Sobel, *Trabelin' On: The Slave Journey to an Afro-Baptist Faith* (Westport, CT: Greenwood Press, 1979); Sterling Stuckey, *Slave Culture: Nationalist Theory and the Foundations of Black America* (New York: Oxford University Press, 1987); Joseph M. Murphy, *Working the Spirit: Ceremonies of the African Diaspora* (Boston: Beacon Press, 1994); and Joseph E. Holloway, *Africanisms in American Culture*.

9. Amiri Baraka, *Blues People* (New York: Morrow, 1963), 16.

10. Thomas C. Oden, *How Africa Shaped the Christian Mind* (Downers Grove, IL: IVP Books, 2007), 10.

11. See Ninian Smart, *Worldviews: Crosscultural Explorations of Human Beliefs* (Upper Saddle River, NJ: Prentice Hall, 2000).

12. Deuteronomy 6:2.

13. 1 Corinthians 15:3.

14. Raboteau, *Slave Religion*, 64.

15. In arguing the continuity of African cultural retentions (Africanisms) within African American religious tradition, see the work of Herskovits, *The Myth of the Negro Past*; Carter G. Woodson, *The History of the Negro Church* (1921; Washington, DC: Associated Publishers, 1992); Lorenzo Turner, *Africanisms in the Gullah Dialect* (Charleston: University of South Carolina Press, 2002); Eugene D. Genovese, *Roll, Jordan, Roll: The World the Slaves Made* (New York: Vintage, 1974); Vincent G. Harding, "Religion and Resistance among Antebellum Negroes, 1800–1860," in *The Making of Black America: Essays in Negro Life and History*, ed. August Meier and

Elliott Rudwick (New York: Athaneum, 1969); Roger Bastide, *The African Religions of Brazil: Toward a Sociology of the Interpenetration of Civilizations*, trans. Helen Sebba (Baltimore: Johns Hopkins University Press, 1978); and Blassingame, *The Slave Community*. Whereas Raboteau's assertions do not represent a full-blown break with this perspective on continuity of Africanisms within the African American religious experience, he does temper the bold overtones indicated by such claims.

16. See Gomez, *Exchanging Our Country's Marks*.

17. Herskovits, *The Myth of the Negro Past*, 214.

18. Søren Kierkegaard, *Journals and Papers*, vol. 18 (1843; Bloomington: Indiana University Press, 1967), 306.

19. DuBois, *The Souls of Black Folk*, 191.

20. For a more thorough depiction of the details surrounding the relationship between death and the Transatlantic Slave Trade, see Vincent Brown, *The Reaper's Garden: Death and Power in the World of Atlantic Slavery* (Cambridge, MA: Harvard University Press, 2008).

21. For further discussion of the concept of death and reincarnation within African traditional religions, see John S. Mbiti, *African Religions and Philosophy* (New York: Praeger, 1969), 83–91, 149–65.

22. Robert Farris Thompson, *The Four Moments of the Sun: Kongo Art in Two Worlds* (Washington, DC: National Gallery of Art, 1981), 186–87; Robert Farris Thompson, *Flash of the Spirit: African and Afro-American Art and Philosophy* (New York: Random House, 1983), 132–39.

23. Suzanne E. Smith, *To Serve the Living: Funeral Directors and the African American Way of Death* (Cambridge, MA: Belknap Press of Harvard, 2010), 19–20.

24. Herskovits, *The Myth of the Negro Past*, 197–98.

25. For examples of retention of African funeral practices, see Ross W. Jamieson, "Material Culture and Social Death: African American Burial Practices," *Historical Archeology* 29, no. 4 (1995): 39–58; and Vincent Brown, *The Reaper's Garden*, 63–66.

26. Karla F. C. Holloway, *Passed On: African American Mourning Stories* (Durham, NC: Duke University Press, 2002); also see Suzanne Smith, T*o Serve the Living*.

27. Karla F. C. Holloway, *Passed On*, 151.

28. Ibid., 155, 175.

29. Ardencie Hall, "New Orleans Jazz Funerals: Transition to the Ancestors" (PhD diss., New York University, 1998).

30. Karla F. C. Holloway, *Passed On*, 170.

31. Winthrop D. Jordan, *White over Black: American Attitudes toward the Negro, 1550–1812* (1968; New York: Norton, 1977); Edmund S. Morgan, *American Slav-*

ery, American Freedom: The Ordeal of Colonial Virginia (New York: Norton, 1975); A. Leon Higginbotham, *In the Matter of Color: Race and the American Legal Process: The Colonial Period* (New York: Oxford University Press, 1978).

32. Jennifer L. Morgan, *Laboring Women: Reproduction and Gender in New World Slavery* (Philadelphia: University of Pennsylvania Press, 2004).

33. See Raboteau, *Slave Religion*.

34. Gayraud S. Wilmore, *Black Religion and Black Radicalism: An Interpretation of the Religious History of African Americans*, 3rd ed. (1972; Maryknoll, NY: Orbis, 1998), 44–48; Margarite Fernández Olmos and Lizabeth Paravisini-Gebert, *Creole Religions of the Caribbean: An Introduction from Vodou and Santería to Obeah and Espiritismo* (New York: New York University Press, 2003).

35. Milton C. Sernett, *Black Religion and American Evangelicalism: White Protestants, Plantation Missions, and the Flowering of Negro Christianity, 1787–1865* (Metuchen, NJ: Scarecrow Press, 1975).

36. Kolchin, *American Slavery*, 55.

37. When considering the cultural exchange between Black Christianity and the mainline church, see Sobel, *Trabelin' On*; Eugene Genovese, *Roll, Jordan, Roll*, 210–19; Raboteau, *Slave Religion*, 48–55, 63; and Donald H. Matthews, *Honoring the Ancestors: An African Cultural Interpretation of Black Religion and Literature* (New York: Oxford University Press, 1998), 3–23.

38. Patricia U. Bonomi, *Under the Cope of Heaven: Religion, Society, and Politics in Colonial America* (New York: Oxford University Press, 2003), 125–26.

39. Woodson, *The History of the Negro Church*, 42.

40. James M. Simms, *The First Colored Baptist Church in North America* (New York: Negro Universities Press, 1969), 71–75.

41. Cedrick May, "John Marrant and the Narrative Construction of an Early Black Methodist Evangelical," *African American Review* 38, no. 4 (Winter 2004): 553–70.

42. Richard Allen, *The Life Experience and Gospel Labors of the Rt. Rev. Richard Allen* (Nashville: Abingdon Press, 1960); Marcia M. Mathews, *Richard Allen* (Baltimore: Helicon, 1963); Carol V. R. George, *Segregated Sabbaths: Richard Allen and the Emergence of Independent Black Churches 1760–1840* (New York: Oxford University Press, 1973); Albert J. Raboteau, *A Fire in the Bones: Reflections on African-American Religious History* (Boston: Beacon Press, 1995).

43. James W. Hood, *One Hundred Years of the African Methodist Episcopal Zion Church* (New York: A.M.E. Zion Book Concern, 1895).

44. Gary B. Nash, *Forging Freedom: The Formation of Philadelphia's Black Community, 1720–1840* (Cambridge, MA: Harvard University Press, 1991).

45. Stephen R. Haynes, *Noah's Curse: The Biblical Justification of American Slavery* (New York: Oxford University Press, 2002); David M. Goldenberg, *The Curse of Ham: Race and Slavery in Early Judaism, Christianity, and Islam* (Princeton, NJ: Princeton University Press, 2003); Elizabeth Fox-Genovese and Eugene D. Genovese, *The Mind of the Master Class: History and Faith in the Southern Slaveholders' Worldview* (New York: Cambridge University Press, 2005).

46. Charles L. Perdue Jr., Thomas E. Barden, and Robert K. Phillips, eds., *Weevils in the Wheat: Interviews with Virginia Ex-Slaves* (1976; Charlottesville: University of Virginia Press, 1991).

47. Herbert Aptheker, *American Negro Slave Revolts* (New York: International Publishers, 1963); Gerald W. Mullin, *Flight and Rebellion: Slave Resistance in Eighteenth-Century Virginia* (New York: Oxford University Press, 1972); Eugene D. Genovese, *From Rebellion to Revolution: Afro-American Slave Revolts in the Making of the Modern World* (Baton Rouge: Louisiana State University Press, 1979); Merton L. Dillon, *Slavery Attacked: Southern Slaves and Their Allies, 1619–1865* (Baton Rouge; Louisiana State University Press, 1990); Douglas R. Egerton, *Gabriel's Rebellion: The Virginia Slave Conspiracies of 1800 and 1802* (Chapel Hill: University of North Carolina Press, 1993); Kenneth S. Greenberg, *Nat Turner: A Slave Rebellion in History and Memory* (New York: Oxford University Press, 2003).

48. David R. Roediger, "And Die in Dixie: Funerals, Death, and Heaven in the Slave Community, 1700–1865," *Massachusetts Review* (1981): 163–83; Sobel, *Trabelin' On*, 187–200; Raboteau, *Slave Religion*, 230–31; Ira Berlin, *Many Thousands Gone: The First Two Centuries of Slavery in North America* (Cambridge, MA: Belknap Press of Harvard University Press, 1998), 60–63, 158; and Suzanne Smith, *To Serve the Living*, 25–27.

49. Eddie S. Glaude Jr., *Exodus!*

50. See DuBois, *The Souls of Black Folk*; Howard Thurman, *Deep River and the Negro Spiritual Speaks of Life and Death* (Richmond, IN: Friends United Press, 1975); and James H. Cone, *The Spirituals and the Blues: An Interpretation* (Maryknoll, NY: Orbis, 1972).

51. Lovell, *Black Song*; John Michael Spencer, *Protest and Praise: Sacred Music of Black Religion* (Minneapolis: Augsburg Fortress, 1990).

52. Wilmore, *Black Religion and Black Radicalism*, 99.

53. Leon F. Litwack, *North of Slavery: The Negro in the Free States* (Chicago: University of Chicago Press, 1961), 212.

54. Evelyn Brooks Higginbotham, *Righteous Discontent: The Women's Movement in the Black Baptist Church, 1880–1920* (Cambridge, MA: Harvard University Press, 1993).

55. "The Free African American Press—*Freedom's Journal*, 1827," The African American Odyssey—Library of Congress, accessed December 21, 2013, memory.loc .gov/ammem/aaohtml/aopart2b.html.

56. Glaude, *Exodus!*, 113, 160–63. For recent works reflecting the interrogation of notions of racial solidarity qua political mobilization, also see Michael Dawson, *Black Visions: The Roots of Contemporary African-American Political Ideologies* (Chicago: University of Chicago Press, 2003); Tommie Shelby, *We Who Are Dark: The Philosophical Foundations of Black Solidarity* (Boston: Belknap Press, 2005); and James Davison Jr., *Sweet Release: The Last Step to Black Freedom* (Amherst, NY: Prometheus, 2008).

57. David W. Blight, ed., *Passages to Freedom: The Underground Railroad in History and Memory* (Washington, DC: Smithsonian Books, 2004); Fergus M. Bordewich, *Bound for Canaan: The Underground Railroad and the War for the Soul of America* (New York: Amistad, 2005).

58. David Walker and Henry Highland Garnet, *Walker's Appeal and Garnet Address* (Nashville: Winston-Derek, 1994), 37.

59. P. J. Staudenraus, *The African Colonization Movement 1816–1865* (New York: Columbia University Press, 1961).

60. Michel-Rolph Trouillot, *Silencing the Past: Power and the Production of History* (Boston: Beacon Press, 1995), 49–53.

61. These and other questions were recently posed by Vincent Caretta, *Equiano, the African: Biography of a Self-Made Man* (New York: Penguin, 2005).

62. For detailed discussion of the various elements of slave religion gleaned from slave narratives, see Cheryl Saunders, *Slavery and Conversion: An Analysis of Ex-Slave Testimony* (ThD thesis, Harvard University, 1985); Riggins Earl, *Dark Symbols, Obscure Signs: God, Self, and Community in the Slave Mind* (Maryknoll, NY: Orbis, 1993); Dwight Hopkins and George Cummings, eds., *Cut Loose Your Stammering Tongue: Black Theology in the Slave Narratives* (Maryknoll, NY: Orbis, 1991). In order to find comprehensive collections of the slave narratives, see also George P. Rawick, ed., *The American Slave: A Composite Autobiography*, 19 vols. (Westport, CT: Greenwood Press, 1972, 1977); Paul D. Escott, *Slavery Remembered: Record of Twentieth-Century Slave Narratives* (Chapel Hill: University of North Carolina Press, 1979); Clifton H. Johnson, ed., *God Struck Me Dead: Voices of Ex-Slaves* (Cleveland: Pilgrim Press, 1993).

63. Steven Mintz, ed., *African American Voices: The Life Cycle of Slavery*, rev. ed. (1993; St. James, NY: Brandywine Press, 1996), 95.

64. Ibid.

65. Ibid.

66. Ibid., 96.

67. Ibid.

68. Toni Morrison, *Beloved* (New York: Random House, 1986).

69. Kenneth M. Stampp, *The Peculiar Institution: Slavery in the Ante-bellum South* (New York: Knopf, 1956).

70. David M. Potter, *The Impending Crisis, 1848–1861* (New York: Harper & Row, 1976); Vincent G. Harding, *There Is a River: The Black Struggle for Freedom in America* (New York: Harcourt Brace Jovanovich, 1981); James M. McPherson, *Battle Cry of Freedom: The Civil War Era* (1988; New York: Oxford University Press, 2003).

71. James M. McPherson, *For Cause and Comrades: Why Men Fought in the Civil War* (New York: Oxford University Press, 1998); David W. Blight, *Race and Reunion: The Civil War in American Memory* (Cambridge, MA: Belknap Press of Harvard University Press, 2002); Mark A. Noll, *The Civil War as a Theological Crisis* (Chapel Hill: University of North Carolina Press, 2006); Harry S. Stout, *Upon the Altar of the Nation: A Moral History of the Civil War* (New York: Penguin, 2007); Chandra Manning, *What This Cruel War Was Over: Soldiers, Slavery, and the Civil War* (New York: Vintage, 2008); Drew G. Faust, *This Republic of Suffering: Death and the American Civil War* (New York: Vintage, 2008).

72. Benjamin Quarles, *The Negro in the Civil War* (Boston: Little, Brown, 1953); James M. McPherson, *The Negro's Civil War: How American Negroes Felt and Acted during the War for the Union* (New York: Pantheon Books, 1965); Dudley Taylor Cornish, *The Sable Arm: Black Troops in the Union Army, 1861–1865* (New York: Norton, 1966); Edwin S. Redkey, ed., *A Grand Army of Black Men: Letters from African-American Soldiers in the Union Army, 1861–1865* (New York: Cambridge University Press, 1992); Andrew Ward, *The Slaves' War: The Civil War in the Words of Former Slaves* (Boston: Mariner Books, 2009).

73. William L. Andrews, *The Oxford Frederick Douglass Reader* (New York: Oxford University Press, 1996), 226.

74. Juan Williams and Quinton Dixie, *This Far by Faith: Stories from the African American Religious Experience* (New York: W. Morrow, 2003), 109.

75. Eugene Genovese, *Roll, Jordan, Roll*, 213.

76. Matthews, *Honoring the Ancestors*, 25; Eugene Genovese, *Roll, Jordan, Roll*, 249.

77. W. E. B. DuBois, *Black Reconstruction in America, 1860–1880* (1935; New York: Free Press, 1998), 122.

78. Ibid., 124.

79. For recent scholarship addressing the ways in which the Civil War effectively transformed how Americans related to death and dying, see Faust, *This Republic of Suffering*; Garry Wills, *Lincoln at Gettysburg: The Words That Remade America* (New York:

Simon & Schuster, 1992), 63–89; Gary Laderman, *The Sacred Remains: American Attitudes toward Death, 1799–1883* (New Haven: Yale University Press, 1996), 104–5; Stout, *Upon the Altar of the Nation*; and Suzanne Smith, *To Serve the Living*, 31–32.

2. MAKING AMERICA AGAIN

1. The "Age of Revolution" commonly refers to a historical period from approximately 1775 to 1848 during which a number of significant revolutionary movements occurred in the Americas and Europe. During this era, there were profound political and cultural transformations within numerous Western societies as they made the transition from absolutist monarchies to constitutionalist nation-states and democratic republics. For more information, see Eric Hobsbawm, *The Age of Revolution, 1789–1848* (New York: Vintage, 1996).

2. See Robin Blackburn, *The Overthrow of Colonial Slavery, 1776–1848* (London: Verso, 1988); Lynn Hunt, *Inventing Human Rights: A History* (New York: W. W. Norton, 2007); Stephanie McCurry, "War, Gender, and Emancipation in the Civil War South," in *Lincoln's Proclamation: Emancipation Reconsidered,* ed. William A Blair and Karen Fisher Younger (Chapel Hill: The University of North Carolina Press, 2009); Christopher Leslie Brown, *Moral Capital: Foundations of British Abolitionism* (Chapel Hill: University of North Carolina Press, 2006), 235–36; Persis Charles, "The Name of the Father: Women, Paternity, and British Rule in Nineteenth-Century Jamaica," *International Labor and Working-Class History* 41 (Spring 1992): 4–48; Myriam Cottias, "Gender and Republican Identity in the French West Indies, 1848–1945," *Slavery & Abolition* 26, no. 2 (2005): 233–45; Elizabeth Colwill, "'Fêtes de l'hymen, fêtes de la liberté': Marriage, Manhood, and Emancipation in Revolutionary Saint-Domingue," in *The World of the Haitian Revolution,* ed. David Patrick Geggus and Norman Fiering (Bloomington: Indiana University Press, 2009), 125–55; Pamela Scully and Diana Paton, eds., *Gender and Slave Emancipation in the Atlantic World* (Durham, NC: Duke University Press, 2005), esp. 13, 155–56; Frederick Cooper, Thomas C. Holt, and Rebecca J. Scott, *Beyond Slavery: Explorations of Race, Labor, and Citizenship in Postemancipation Societies* (Chapel Hill: University of North Carolina Press, 2000), 112–20; and Amy Dru Stanley, "Instead of Waiting for the Thirteenth Amendment: The War Power, Slave Marriage, and Inviolate Human Rights" *American Historical Review* (June 2010): 732–65.

3. Lincoln and Mamiya, *The Black Church in the African American Experience*, 8.

4. Sydney E. Ahlstrom, *A Religious History of the American People* (New Haven, CT: Yale University Press, 1973), 710.

5. Raboteau, *A Fire in the Bones:*, 59–63, 71–72, 169, and 187.

6. Darlene Clark Hine, William C. Hine, and Stanley Harrold, *The African-American Odyssey* (Upper Saddle River, NJ: Prentice Hall, 2000), 265.

7. Quoted in Hine, Hine, and Harrold, *The African American Odyssey,* 265.

8. Leon F. Litwack, *Been in the Storm: The Aftermath of Slavery* (New York: Vintage, 1979), 457.

9. Joe M. Richardson, *Christian Reconstruction: The American Missionary Association and Southern Blacks, 1861–1890* (Athens: University of Georgia Press, 1986).

10. Albert J. Raboteau, *Canaan Land: A Religious History of African Americans* (New York: Oxford University Press, 2001). See also Ronald E. Butchart, *Northern Schools, Southern Blacks, and Reconstruction: Freedmen's Educaton, 1862–1875* (Westport, CT: Greenwood Press, 1980); Robert C. Morris, *Reading, 'Riting, and Reconstruction: The Education of Freedmen in the South, 1861–1870* (Chicago: University of Chicago Press, 1981); James D. Anderson, *The Education of Blacks in the South, 1860–1935* (Chapel Hill: University of North Carolina Press, 1988).

11. Andrew Billingsley, *Mighty Like a River: The Black Church and Social Reform* (New York: Oxford University Press, 1999), 68–70.

12. Hine, Hine, and Harrold, *The African-American Odyssey,* 341.

13. DuBois, *The Souls of Black Folk,* 149.

14. James M. Washington, *Frustrated Fellowship: The Black Baptist Quest for Social Power* (Macon, GA: Mercer University Press, 1986).

15. Cheryl Townsend Gilkes, *If It Wasn't for the Women . . .: Black Women's Experience and Womanist Culture in Church and Community* (Maryknoll, NY: Orbis Books 2001); Daphne C. Wiggins, *Righteous Content: Black Women's Perspectives of Church and Faith* (New York: New York University Press, 2005).

16. Milton C. Sernett, ed., *African American Religious History: A Documentary Witness* (Durham, NC: Duke University Press, 2000), 173.

17. William L. Andrews, ed., *Sisters of the Spirit: Three Black Women's Autobiographies of the Nineteenth Century* (Bloomington: Indiana University Press, 1986); Bettye Collier-Thomas, ed., *Daughters of Thunder: Black Women Preachers and Their Sermons, 1850–1979* (San Francisco: Jossey-Bass, 1998).

18. Evelyn Brooks Higginbotham, *Righteous Discontent.*

19. Benjamin E. Mays, *Born to Rebel: An Autobiography* (New York: Scribners, 1971), 14, 15.

20. Hine, Hine, and Harrold, *The African-American Odyssey,* 343.

21. Richard Wright, *Uncle Tom's Children* (1938; New York: Harper Perennial, 1998).

22. Wilmore, *Black Religion and Black Radicalism,* 163–95.

23. Hine, Hine, and Harrold, *The African American Odyssey,* 343.

24. Edwin S. Redkey, *Black Exodus: Black Nationalist and Back-to-Africa Movements, 1890–1910* (New Haven, CT: Yale University Press, 1969); Stephen W. Angell, *Bishop Henry McNeal Turner and African-American Religion in the South* (Knoxville: University of Tennessee Press, 1992).

25. Hine, Hine, and Harrold, *The African-American Odyssey*, 343.

26. Martha Simmons, Frank A. Thomas, and Gardener C. Taylor, eds., *Preaching with Sacred Fire: An Anthology of African American Sermons, 1750 to Present* (New York: Norton, 2010), 347.

27. Anna Julia Cooper, *A Voice from the South* (1892; repr., New York: Oxford University Press, 1990).

28. Barbara Welter, "The Cult of True Womanhood, 1820–1860," *American Quarterly* 18, no. 2 part 1 (Summer 1966): 151–74.

29. Booker T. Washington, *A New Negro for a New Century* (1900; New York: Arno Press, 1969).

30. Robert Gregg, *Sparks from the Anvil of Oppression: Philadelphia's African Methodists and Southern Migrants, 1890–1940* (Philadelphia: Temple University Press, 1993); Milton C. Sernett, *Bound for the Promised Land: African American Religion and the Great Migration* (Durham, NC: Duke University Press, 1997); Wallace D. Best, *Passionately Human, No Less Divine: Religion and Culture in Black Chicago, 1915–1952* (Princeton, NJ: Princeton University Press, 2005).

31. Michael W. Harris, *The Rise of Gospel Blues: The Music of Thomas Andrew Dorsey in the Urban Church* (New York: Oxford University Press, 1992).

32. Vinson Synan, *The Holiness-Pentecostal Tradition: Charismatic Movements in the Twentieth Century* (1971; Grand Rapids: Eerdmans, 1997); Ithiel C. Clemmons, *Bishop C. H. Mason and the Roots of the Church of God in Christ* (Bakersfield, CA: Pneuma Life Pub., 1996); Cheryl J. Sanders, *Saints in Exile: The Holiness-Pentecostal Experience in African American Religion and Culture* (New York: Oxford University Press, 1996).

33. C. Vann Woodward, *The Strange Career of Jim Crow* (New York: Oxford University Press, 1955); Jerrold M. Packard, *American Nightmare: The History of Jim Crow* (New York: St. Martin's Press, 2002); Richard Wormser, *The Rise and Fall of Jim Crow* (New York: St. Martin's Press, 2003).

34. Billingsley, *Mighty Like a River*, 11–12.

35. Carl T. Rowan, *Dream Makers, Dream Breakers: The World of Justice Thurgood Marshall* (Boston: Little, Brown, 1993); Mark V. Tushnet, *Making Civil Rights Law: Thurgood Marshall and the Supreme Court, 1936–1961* (New York: Oxford University Press, 1994); Juan Williams, *Thurgood Marshall: American Revolutionary* (New York: Times Books, 1998).

36. Richard Kluger, *Simple Justice: The History of Brown v. Board of Education and Black America's Struggle for Equality* (New York: Knopf, 1975); Derrick A. Bell, *Silent Covenants: Brown v. Board of Education and the Unfulfilled Hopes for Racial Reform* (New York: Oxford University Press, 2004); Charles J. Ogletree Jr., *All Deliberate Speed: Reflections on the First Half Century of Brown v. Board of Education* (New York: Norton, 2004); Michael J. Klarman, *From Jim Crow to Civil Rights: The Supreme Court and the Struggle for Racial Equality* (New York: Oxford University Press, 2004).

37. "Black, White, and Brown," PBS News Hour (May 12, 2004), accessed December 20, 2013, http://www.pbs.org/newshour/bb/law/jan-june04/brown_05-12 .html.

38. Taylor Branch, *Parting the Waters: America in the King Years, 1954–63* (New York: Simon & Schuster, 1988), 120, 122–23, 127, 130, and 137; Amanda Dawkins, "'Unsung hero' of boycott paved way for Parks," *The Huntsville Times*, February 7, 2005; and Phillip House, *Claudette Colvin: Twice Toward Justice* (New York: Farrar, Straus and Giroux, 2009), 62, 99.

39. Quoted in Juan Williams, *Eyes on the Prize: America's Civil Rights Years, 1954-1965* (New York: Penguin, 1988), 64.

40. Martin Luther King Jr., *Stride Toward Freedom: The Montgomery Story* (New York: Harper, 1958); Branch, *Parting the Waters*; Harvard Sitkoff, *The Struggle for Black Equality, 1954–1992* (1981; New York: Hill and Wang, 1993); Stewart Burns, *Daybreak of Freedom: The Montgomery Bus Boycott* (Chapel Hill: University of North Carolina Press, 1997); Michael Eric Dyson, *I May Not Get There with You: The True Martin Luther King, Jr.* (New York: Free Press, 2000).

41. For more comprehensive discussion of the development of the civil rights movement during the late 1950s and early 1960s, see Adam Fairclough, *To Redeem the Soul of America: The Southern Christian Leadership Conference and Martin Luther King, Jr.* (Athens: University of Georgia Press, 1987); Allen J. Matusow, "From Civil Rights to Black Power: The Case of SNCC, 1960–1966," in *Twentieth Century America: Recent Interpretations*, ed. Barton J. Bernstein and Allen J. Matusow (New York: Harcourt, Brace and World, 1969), 531–66; Howard Zinn, *SNCC: The New Abolitionists* (Boston: Beacon Press, 1964); Clayborne Carson, *In Struggle: SNCC and the Black Awakening of the 1960s* (Cambridge, MA: Harvard University Press, 1981); Emily Schottenfeld Stoper, "The Student Nonviolent Coordinating Committee" (PhD diss., Harvard University, 1968); Inge Powell Bell, *CORE and the Strategy of Nonviolence* (New York: Random House, 1968); William Gellerman, *My CORE Program Experience* (Ithaca, NY: Cornell University Press, 1965); August Meier and Elliott Rudwick, *CORE: A Study in the Civil Rights Movement, 1942–1968* (New York: Oxford University Press, 1973); Bayard Rustin, *Down the Line* (Chicago: Quadrangle Books, 1971); Floyd McKissick, *Three-Fifths of a Man* (New York: Macmillan, 1969); James Farmer, *Freedom, When?* (New York: Random House, 1966); Bayard Rustin, *Strategies for Freedom: The Changing Patterns of Black Protest* (New York: Columbia

University Press, 1976); Cleveland Sellers with Robert Terrell, *The River of No Return: The Autobiography of a Black Militant and the Life and Death of SNCC* (New York: William Morrow, 1973); James Forman, *The Making of Black Revolutionaries* (New York: Macmillan, 1972); and Mays, *Born to Rebel*.

42. James H. Cone, *Martin & Malcolm & America: A Dream or a Nightmare* (Maryknoll, NY: Orbis Books, 1992).

43. For a representative sample of scholarship on Malcolm X, see Manning Marable, *Malcolm X: A Life of Reinvention* (New York: Penguin Books, 2011); Michael Eric Dyson, *Making Malcolm: The Myth and Meaning of Malcolm X* (New York: Oxford University Press, 1996); Joe Wood, ed., *Malcolm X: In Our Own Image* (New York: St. Martin's Press, 1992); George Breitman, ed., *Malcolm X Speaks* (New York: Grove Press, 1966), and *By Any Means Necessary* (New York: Pathfinder Press, 1970); Peter L. Goldman, *The Death and Life of Malcolm X* (New York: Harper and Row, 1973); George Breitman, *The Last Year of Malcolm X: The Evolution of a Revolutionary* (New York: Merit Publishers, 1965); Ossie Davis, "Why I Eulogized Malcolm X," *Negro Digest 15* (February 1966): 64–66; Colin Macinnes, "Malcolm, The Lost Hero," *Negro Digest 16* (May 1967): 4–5; William Keorapeste Kgositsile, "Brother Malcolm and the Black Revolution," *Negro Digest* 18 (November 1968): 4–10; C. Eric Lincoln, "Meaning of Malcolm X," *Christian Century* 82 (April 7, 1965): 431–33; Tom Kahn and Bayard Rustin, "The Ambiguous Legacy of Malcolm X," *Dissent* 12 (Spring 1965): 188–92; and Jigs Gardner, "The Murder of Malcolm X," *Monthly Review* 16 (April 1965): 802–5.

44. See Branch, *Parting the Waters*; Taylor Branch, *Pillar of Fire: America in the King Years 1963–65* (New York: Simon & Schuster, 1998); Taylor Branch, *At Canaan's Edge: America in the King Years, 1965–68* (New York: Simon & Schuster, 2006); Dyson, *I May Not Get There with You*, and Michael Eric Dyson, *April 4, 1968: Martin Luther King, Jr.'s Death and How It Changed America* (New York: Basic Civitas Books, 2009); Clayborne Carson, ed. *The Autobiography of Martin Luther King, Jr.* (New York: Grand Central Publishing, 2001); Richard Lischer, *The Preacher King: Martin Luther King, Jr. and the Word That Moved America* (New York: Oxford University Press, 1997); Lewis V. Baldwin, *The Voice of Conscience: The Church in the Mind of Martin Luther King, Jr.* (New York: Oxford University Press, 2010), *Never to Leave Us Alone: The Prayer Life of Martin Luther King Jr.* (Minneapolis: Fortress, 2010), *The Legacy of Martin Luther King, Jr.: The Boundaries of Law, Politics, and Religion* (Notre Dame, IN: University of Notre Dame Press, 2002), *To Make the Wounded Whole: The Cultural Legacy of Martin Luther King, Jr.* (Minneapolis: Fortress, 1992), and *There Is a Balm in Gilead: The Cultural Roots of Martin Luther King, Jr.* (Minneapolis: Fortress, 1991); Vincent Harding, *Martin Luther King: The Inconvenient Hero* (Maryknoll, NY: Orbis Books, 1996); James M. Washington, ed., *A Testament of Hope: The Essential Writings and Speeches of Martin Luther King, Jr.* (New York: Harper San Francisco, 1991); David J. Garrow, *Bearing the Cross: Martin Luther King, Jr., and the Southern Christian Leadership Conference*

(New York: HarperCollins, 1986); Stephen B. Oates, *Let the Trumpet Sound: A Life of Martin Luther King, Jr.* (New York: Harper Perennial, 1994); Marshall Frady, *Martin Luther King, Jr.: A Life* (New York: Penguin Books, 2005); David Levering Lewis, *King: A Critical Biography* (New York: Praeger, 1970); James Alonzo Bishop, *The Days of Martin Luther King, Jr.* (New York: Putnam, 1971); Lerone Bennett, *What Manner of Man: A Biography of Martin Luther King, Jr.* (Chicago: Johnson, 1964); and Laurence Dunbar Reddick, *Crusader without Violence: A Biography of Martin Luther King, Jr.* (New York: Harper and Row, 1959).

45. Joseph R. Washington, *Black Religion: The Negro and Christianity in the United States* (Boston: Beacon Press, 1964), 3.

46. August Meier, "The Conservative Militant," in *Martin Luther King, Jr.: A Profile*, ed. C. Eric Lincoln (New York: Hill and Wang, 1970), 144–56.

47. See Lewis V. Baldwin, *The Legacy of Martin Luther King, Jr., To Make the Wounded Whole*, and *There Is a Balm in Gilead*; Robert M. Franklin, "Religious Belief and Political Activism in Black America," *Journal of Religious Thought* 43 (Fall-Winter 1986–87); and Raboteau, *A Fire in the Bones*.

48. Lischer, *The Preacher King*, 221.

49. Garrow, *Bearing the Cross*.

50. Sudarshan Kapur, *Raising Up a Prophet: The African-American Encounter with Gandhi* (Boston: Beacon Press, 1992).

51. Carson, *In Struggle*.

52. Fairclough, *To Redeem the Soul of America*.

53. Branch, *Pillar of Fire*.

54. Martin Luther King Jr., *Why We Can't Wait* (1963; New York: Signet Classic, 2000).

55. King, *Why We Can't Wait*, 69.

56. Ibid., 81.

57. Jervis Anderson, *Bayard Rustin: Troubles I've Seen: A Biography* (New York: HarperCollins, 1997); Daniel Levine, *Bayard Rustin and the Civil Rights Movement* (New Brunswick, NJ: Rutgers University Press, 2000); John D'Emilio, *Lost Prophet: The Life and Times of Bayard Rustin* (New York: Free Press, 2003); and Devon W. Carbado and Donald Weise, eds., *Time on Two Crosses: The Collected Writings of Bayard Rustin* (San Francisco: Cleis Press, 2003).

58. James M. Washington, *A Testament of Hope*, 231–44.

59. Thomas R. West and James W. Mooney, eds., *To Redeem a Nation: A History and Anthology of the American Civil Rights Movement* (St. James, NY: Brandywine Press, 1993), 153–54.

60. James M. Washington, *A Testament of Hope*, 651–53.

61. Ibid., 279–86.

62. Kwame Ture (formerly known as Stokely Carmichael) and Charles V. Hamilton, *Black Power: The Politics of Liberation in America* (New York: Vintage Books, 1967); Manning Marable, *Race, Reform and Rebellion: The Second Reconstruction in Black America, 1945–1992,* 2nd ed. (Jackson: University Press of Mississippi, 1991); William L. Van Deburg, *New Day in Babylon: The Black Power Movement and American Culture, 1965–1975* (Chicago: University of Chicago Press, 1992); Peniel E. Joseph, *Waiting 'Til the Midnight Hour: A Narrative History of Black Power in America* (New York: Henry Holt, 2006).

63. Charles Marsh, *The Beloved Community: How Faith Shapes Social Justice, from the Civil Rights Movement to Today* (New York: Basic Books, 2005); Branch, *At Canaan's Edge.*

64. Henry H. Mitchell, *Black Preaching: The Recovery of a Powerful Art* (Nashville: Abingdon Press, 1990).

65. Clarence Taylor, *The Black Churches of Brooklyn* (New York: Columbia University Press, 1994).

66. David L. Chappell, *A Stone of Hope: Prophetic Religion and the Death of Jim Crow* (Chapel Hill: University of North Carolina Press, 2004).

67. Clarence Taylor, "African American Religious Leadership and the Civil Rights Movement," *History Now: American History Online* 8, The Gilder Lehrman Institute of American History, June 2006, accessed January 1, 2014, http://www.gilderlehrman.org/history-by-era/civil-rights-movement/essays/african-american-religious-leadership-and-civil-rights-m.

68. Matthew 25:34-46.

69. Belinda Robnett, *How Long? How Long?: African-American Women in the Struggle for Civil Rights* (New York: Oxford University Press, 1997); Charles Marsh, *God's Long Summer: Stories of Faith and Civil Rights* (Princeton, NJ: Princeton University Press, 1997); Joanne Grant, *Ella Baker: Freedom Bound* (New York: Wiley, 1998); Rosetta E. Ross, *Witnessing and Testifying: Black Women, Religion, and Civil Rights* (Minneapolis: Fortress Press, 2003); Barbara Ransby, *Ella Baker and the Black Freedom Movement: A Radical Democratic Vision* (Chapel Hill: University of North Carolina Press, 2003).

70. Henry Hampton and Steve Fayer, eds., *Voices of Freedom: An Oral History of the Civil Rights Movement from the 1950s through the 1980s* (New York: Bantam Books, 1990); Vicki L. Crawford, Jacqueline Anne Rouse, and Barbara Woods, eds., *Women in the Civil Rights Movement: Trailblazers and Torchbearers, 1941–1965* (Brooklyn, NY: Carlson, 1990); John Dittmer, *Local People: The Struggle for Civil Rights in Mississippi* (Urbana: University of Illinois Press, 1994); Charles M. Payne,

I've Got the Light of Freedom: The Organizing Tradition and the Mississippi Freedom Struggle (Berkeley: University of California Press, 1995); Robnett, *How Long? How Long?*; Deborah Gray White, *Too Heavy a Load: Black Women in Defense of Themselves, 1894–1994* (New York: Norton, 1999); Ross, *Witnessing and Testifying.*

71. Alexander Bloom, ed., *Long Time Gone: Sixties America Then and Now* (New York: Oxford University Press, 2001), 18.

3. WE HAVE BEEN BELIEVERS IN THE NEW JERUSALEM

1. Margaret Walker, "We Have Been Believers," in *This Is My Century: New and Collected Poems* (Athens: University of Georgia Press, 2013), 9–10.

2. See "State of the Dream 2011: Austerity for Whom?," accessed December 22, 2013, http://www.faireconomy.org/files/State_of_the_Dream_2011.pdf.

3. Eugene Robinson, *Disintegration: The Splintering of Black America* (New York: Doubleday Books, 2010).

4. "A Religious Portrait of African-Americans," The Pew Forum on Religion & Public Life, January 30, 2009, accessed December 22, 2013, http://www.pewforum.org/A-Religious-Portrait-of-African-Americans.aspx#1.

5. Ibid.

6. Ture and Hamilton, *Black Power.* For a comprehensive survey of the history of the Black Power movement, see Joseph, *Waiting 'Til the Midnight Hour.*

7. Robin D. G. Kelley, *Freedom Dreams: The Black Radical Imagination* (Boston: Beacon, 2002), 120.

8. James H. Cone, *A Black Theology of Liberation* (Maryknoll, NY: Orbis Books, 2010), 1.

9. J. Deotis Roberts, *Liberation and Reconciliation: A Black Theology* (Philadelphia: Westminster Press, 1971), 26.

10. Ibid., 27.

11. Josiah Young, *Pan-African Theology: Providence and the Legacies of the Ancestors* (Trenton, NJ: Africa World Press, 1992); James Evans, *We Have Been Believers: An African American Systematic Theology* (1992; Minneapolis: Fortress Press, 2012); Noel Erskine, *Decolonizing Theology: A Caribbean Perspective* (1981; Trenton, NJ: Africa World Press, 1998); George Cummings, *A Common Journey: Black Theology and Latin American Liberation Theology* (Maryknoll, NY: Orbis Books, 1989). Without question, Dwight Hopkins has been the most prolific Black liberation theologian of his generational cohort, with the publication of works such as *Black Theology USA and South Africa: Politics, Culture, and Liberation* (1989; Eugene, OR: Wipf & Stock, 2005); *Shoes That Fit Our Feet: Sources for a Constructive Black Theology* (Maryknoll,

NY: Orbis Books, 1993); *Down, Up, and Over: Slave Religion and Black Theology* (Minneapolis: Fortress Press, 1999); *Head and Heart: Black Theology—Past, Present, and Future* (New York: Palgrave Macmillan, 2002); *Introducing Black Theology of Liberation* (Maryknoll, NY: Orbis Books, 1999); and *Being Human: Race, Culture, and Religion* (Minneapolis: Fortress Press, 2005). For a more general overall survey of this topic, see also Juan M. Floyd-Thomas, "Liberation: A Definition," in *The Oxford Handbook of African American Theology*, ed. Anthony B. Pinn and Katie G. Cannon (New York: Oxford University Press, 2013).

12. "The Story Behind the Foot Washing at the 1994 'Mephis Miracle,'" Flower Pentecostal Heritage Center, July 13, 2011, accessed December 15, 2013, http://ifphc.wordpress.com/2011/07/13/donaldevans/.

13. The classic definition of womanism can be found in Alice Walker, *In Search of Our Mothers' Gardens* (San Diego: Harcourt, 1983), xi–xii.

14. Jualyne Dodson and Cheryl Townsend Gilkes, "Something Within: Social Change and Collective Endurance in the Sacred World of Black Christian Women," in *Women and Religion in America*, vol. 3, ed. Rosemary Radford Ruether and Rosemary Skinner (San Francisco: Harper and Row, 1986), 80–130. This examination of Black women's roles within church and society is later advanced in Gilkes, *If It Wasn't for the Women . . .*

15. Emilie M. Townes, "Voices of the Spirit: Womanist Methodologies in the Theological Disciplines," *The Womanist* 1, no. 1 (Summer 1994): 1.

16. Kelly Brown Douglas, *The Black Christ* (Maryknoll, NY: Orbis Books, 1994), 99.

17. Katie G. Cannon, *Katie's Canon: Womanism and the Soul of the Black Community* (New York: Continuum, 1995), 47.

18. Ibid.

19. Delores S. Williams, *Sisters in the Wilderness: The Challenge of Womanist God-Talk* (Maryknoll, NY: Orbis Books, 1993), 175.

20. Jacquelyn Grant, "Womanist Theology: Black Women's Experience as a Source for Doing Theology, with Special Reference to Christology," in *Black Theology: A Documentary History*, vol. 2, 1980–1992, ed. James H. Cone and Gayraud S. Wilmore (Maryknoll, NY: Orbis Books, 1993), 278.

21. See Emilie M. Townes, ed., *A Troubling in My Soul: Womanist Perspectives on Evil and Suffering* (Maryknoll, NY: Orbis, 1993); Stacey M. Floyd-Thomas, ed., *Deeper Shades of Purple: Womanism in Religion and Society* (New York: New York University Press, 2006); Layli Phillips, ed., *The Womanist Reader: The First Quarter Century of Womanist Thought* (London: Routledge, 2006); and Katie Geneva Cannon, Emilie M. Townes, and Angela D. Sims, eds., *Womanist Theological Ethics: A Reader* (Louisville, KY: Westminster John Knox Press, 2011).

22. "Incarcerated America," Human Rights Watch, Figure 1, "Race, Population, and Incarceration," April 2003, accessed December 22, 2013, http://www.hrw.org/backgrounder/usa/incarceration/.

23. Tony Samara, "Prisons, Punishment, and Profiteers," accessed December 22, 2013, http://louisville.edu/journal/workplace/issue6/samara.html.

24. "Felony Disenfranchisement Laws in the United States," The Sentencing Project, September 2005, accessed December 22, 2013, http://www.sentencing project.org/detail/publication.cfm?publication_id=15.

25. "Schools and Prisons: Fifty Years After *Brown v. Board of Education,*" The Sentencing Project, accessed December 22, 2013, http://www.sentencingproject.org/Admin/Documents/publications/rd_brownvboard.pdf.

26. Samara, "Prisons, Punishment, and Profiteers."

27. "Schools and Prisons."

28. "US Constitution—13th Amendment," Legal Information Institute, accessed December 26, 2013, http://www.law.cornell.edu/constitution/amendmentxiii.

29. DuBois, *The Souls of Black Folk*, 140.

30. Michelle Alexander, *The New Jim Crow: Mass Incarceration in the Age of Colorblindness* (New York: The New Press, 2012).

31. Jonathan L. Walton, *Watch This!: The Ethics and Aesthetics of Black Televangelism* (New York: New York University Press, 2009), 2.

32. W. E. B. DuBois, *The Philadelphia Negro: A Social Study* (1899; Philadelphia: University of Pennsylvania Press, 1996); W. E. B. DuBois, *The Negro Church: Report of a Social Study Made under the Direction of Atlanta University* (1903; Walnut Creek, CA: Altamira Press, 2003).

33. Paul Tillich, *Dynamics of Faith* (New York: Harper, 1957).

34. Anthony B. Pinn, *The Black Church in the Post-Civil Rights Era* (Maryknoll, NY: Orbis Books, 1999), 139.

35. Walton, *Watch This!*, xi. See also Shayne Lee, *T. D. Jakes: America's New Preacher* (New York: New York University Press, 2005); Stephanie Y. Mitchem, *Name It and Claim It?: Prosperity Preaching in the Black Church* (Cleveland, OH: Pilgrim Press, 2007); Shayne Lee and Phillip Luke Sinitiere, *Holy Mavericks: Evangelical Innovators and the Spiritual Marketplace* (New York: New York University Press, 2009); Sandra L. Barnes, *Black Megachurch Culture* (New York: Peter Lang Publishing, 2010); and Tamelyn N. Tucker-Worgs, *The Black Megachurch: Theology, Gender, and the Politics of Public Engagement* (Waco, TX: Baylor University Press, 2011).

36. For further details and analysis regarding how African Americans as a whole are suffering disproportionately in this recessionary economic cycle across numerous economic indicators, please see Meizhu Lui et al., *The Color of Wealth: The Story Be-*

hind the U.S. Racial Wealth Divide (New York: New Press, 2006); Algernon Austin, "Reversal of Fortune: Economic Gains of 1990s Overturned for African Americans from 2000–07," Economic Policy Institute, EPI Briefing Paper #220, September 18, 2008, accessed December 28, 2013, http://epi.3cdn.net/f205db387e418862d6 _c5m6bhw0j.pdf; Amaad Rivera, Brenda Cotto-Escalera, Anisha Desai, Jeannette Huezo, and Dedrick Muhammad, "State of the Dream 2010: Drained—Jobless and Foreclosed in Communities of Color," United for a Fair Economy, January 13, 2010, accessed December 29, 2013, http://www.faireconomy.org/files/SoD_2010 _Drained_Report.pdf; Luke Reidenbach and Christian E. Weller, "The State of Minorities in 2010: Minorities Are Suffering Disproportionately in the Recession," Center for American Progress, January 15, 2010, accessed December 29, 2013, http://www.americanprogress.org/issues/2010/01/state_of_minorities.html; and the March 2010 report entitled "Understanding the Economy: Long-Term Unemployment in the African American Community," Joint Economic Committee chaired by Representative Carolyn B. Maloney (D-NY), Chair, March 2010, accessed December 29, 2013, http://jec.senate.gov/public/?a=Files.Serve&File_id=f7a324ea-4998 -4a96-aeea-0265a3a68aae.

37. In his essay entitled "The Problem of Amusement," W. E. B. DuBois argues that the Black Church

> is a broader, deeper, and more comprehensive social organism than the churches of white Americans. The [Black] church is not simply an organism for the propagation of religion; it is the centre of the social, intellectual, and religious life of an organized group of people. It provides social intercourse, it provides amusements of various kinds, it serves as a newspaper and intelligence bureau, it supplants the theatre, it directs the picnic and excursion, it furnishes the music, it introduces the stranger to the community, it serves as the lyceum, library, and lecture bureau—it is, in fine, the central organ of the organized life of [African Americans] for amusement, relaxation, instruction, and religion. (Quoted in Phil Zuckerman, *Du Bois on Religion* [Walnut Creek, CA: Alta Mira Press, 2000], 21.)

38. Manning Marable, *Blackwater: Historical Studies in Race, Class Consciousness, and Revolution* (Niwot: University Press of Colorado, 1981), 43.

39. In his classic survey of African American religious history, Gayraud Wilmore argues that, by increasingly orienting themselves toward seeking acceptance into mainstream white society, the mainline Black churches largely ceded their concern for cultural pride, racial solidarity, and political leadership to secular activists and intellectuals. This phenomenon eventually resulted in what Wilmore deems the "deradicalization of the black church" and the "de-Christianization of black radicalism" (Wilmore, *Black Religion and Black Radicalism*).

40. Benjamin E. Mays and Joseph W. Nicholson, *The Negro's Church* (New York: Arno Press, 1969), 59.

41. E. Franklin Frazier, *The Negro Church in America* (New York: Schocken Books, 1964), 51, 72–73.

42. Tillich, *Dynamics of Faith*, 1–12.

43. For a rich and insightful primer on the theological and sociological impact of prosperity preaching within the Black Church tradition, see Mitchem, *Name It and Claim It?*.

44. Adolph L. Reed Jr., *The Jesse Jackson Phenomenon: The Crisis of Purpose in Afro-American Politics* (New Haven, CT: Yale University Press, 1986).

45. Raboteau, *Canaan Land*. See also Billingsley, *Mighty Like a River*; Fredrick C. Harris, *Something Within: Religion in African-American Political Activism* (New York: Oxford University Press, 1999); R. Drew Smith, ed., *New Day Begun: African American Churches and Civic Culture in Post-Civil Rights America* (Durham, NC: Duke University Press, 2003).

46. In addition to President Obama's own monographs, *Dreams from My Father* (1995; New York: Broadway, 2004) and *The Audacity of Hope: Thoughts on Reclaiming the American Dream* (New York: Vintage, 2006), also see T. Denean Sharpley-Whiting, ed., *The Speech: Race and Barack Obama's "A More Perfect Union"* (New York: Bloomsbury, 2009); Thomas J. Sugrue, *Not Even Past: Barack Obama and the Burden of Race* (Princeton, NJ: Princeton University Press, 2009); David Remnick, *The Bridge: The Life and Rise of Barack Obama* (New York: Knopf, 2010); Jonathan Alter, *The Promise: President Obama, Year One* (New York: Simon & Schuster, 2010); William Jelani Cobb, *The Substance of Hope: Barack Obama and the Paradox of Progress* (New York: Walker Books, 2010); Michael Tesler and David O. Sears, *Obama's Race: The 2008 Election and the Dream of a Post-Racial America* (Chicago: University of Chicago Press, 2010); Mary Frances Berry and Josh Gottheimer, *Power in Words: The Stories behind Barack Obama's Speeches, from the State House to the White House* (Boston: Beacon Press, 2010); Peniel E. Joseph, *Dark Days, Bright Nights: From Black Power to Barack Obama* (New York: Basic Civitas Books, 2010); James T. Kloppenberg, *Reading Obama: Dreams, Hope, and the American Political Tradition* (Princeton, NJ: Princeton University Press, 2011); Randall Kennedy, *The Persistence of the Color Line: Racial Politics and the Obama Presidency* (New York: Vintage, 2011); Fredrick Harris, *The Price of the Ticket: Barack Obama and Rise and Decline of Black Politics* (New York: Oxford University Press, 2012); Jodi Kantor, *The Obamas* (New York: Little, Brown, 2012); Janny Scott, *A Singular Woman: The Untold Story of Barack Obama's Mother* (New York: Penguin, 2011); Sally H. Jacobs, *The Other Barack: The Bold and Reckless Life of President Obama's Father* (New York: Public Affairs, 2011); David Maraniss, *Barack Obama: The Story* (New York: Simon & Schuster, 2012); and Jonathan Alter, *The Center Holds: Obama and His Enemies* (New York: Simon & Schuster, 2013).

47. Kloppenberg, *Reading Obama*, xxxvii.

48. Ibid., 83.

49. Obama, *Dreams from My Father*, 426–27.

50. Billingsley, *Mighty Like a River*, 170–81; Sharpley-Whiting, *The Speech*; Jeremiah A. Wright Jr., *A Sankofa Moment: The History of Trinity United Church of Christ* (Dallas: St. Paul Press, 2010); Susan Williams Smith, *The Book of Jeremiah: The Life and Ministry of Jeremiah A. Wright Jr.* (Cleveland, OH: Pilgrim Press, 2013); and Carl A. Grant and Shelby J. Grant, *The Moment: Barack Obama, Jeremiah Wright, and the Firestorm at Trinity United Church of Christ* (Lanham, MD: Rowman and Littlefield, 2013).

CPSIA information can be obtained
at www.ICGtesting.com
Printed in the USA
LVHW091300240821
695987LV00013B/133